PIANO • VOCAL • GUITAR

HE IS EXALTED
MUSIC FOR BLENDED WORSHIP

ISBN 0-634-06834-2

HAL•LEONARD®
CORPORATION
7777 W. BLUEMOUND RD. P.O. BOX 13819 MILWAUKEE, WI 53213

Visit Hal Leonard Online at
www.halleonard.com

CONTENTS

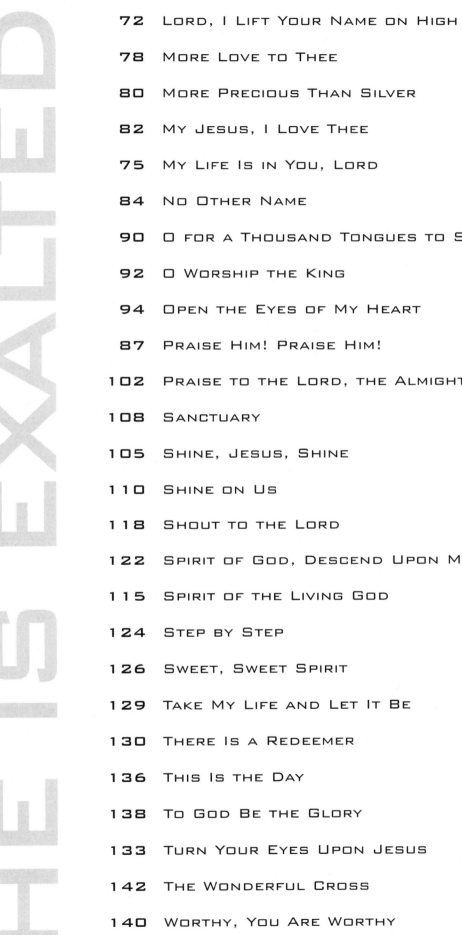

HE IS EXALTED

ALL CREATURES OF OUR GOD AND KING

Words by FRANCIS OF ASSISI
Music from *Geistliche Kirchengesäng*

With dignity

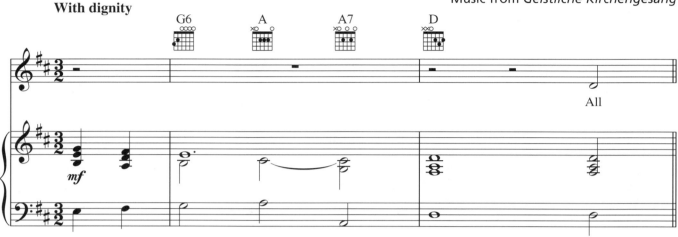

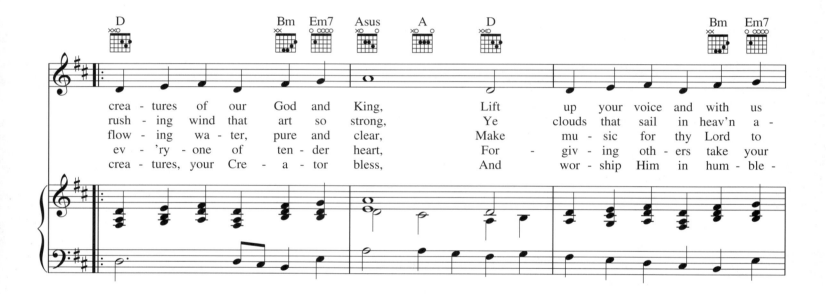

crea- tures of our God and King, Lift up your voice and with us
rush- ing wind that art so strong, Ye clouds that sail in heav'n a-
flow- ing wa- ter, pure and clear, Make mu- sic for thy Lord to
ev- 'ry- one of ten- der heart, For- giv- ing oth- ers take your
crea- tures, your Cre- a- tor bless, And wor- ship Him in hum- ble-

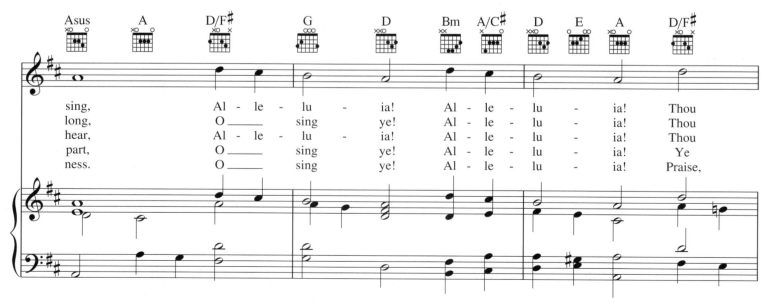

sing, Al- le- lu- ia! Al- le- lu- ia! Thou
long, O sing ye! Al- le- lu- ia! Thou
hear, Al- le- lu- ia! Al- le- lu- ia! Thou
part, O sing ye! Al- le- lu- ia! Ye
ness. O sing ye! Al- le- lu- ia! Praise,

ALL HAIL THE POWER OF JESUS' NAME

Words by EDWARD PERRONET
Music by OLIVER HOLDEN

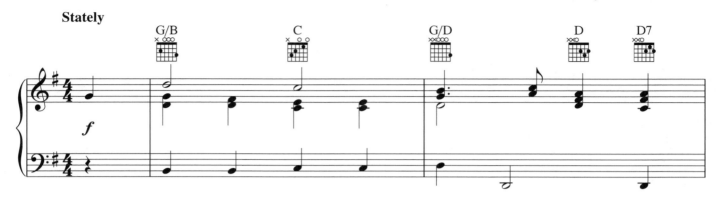

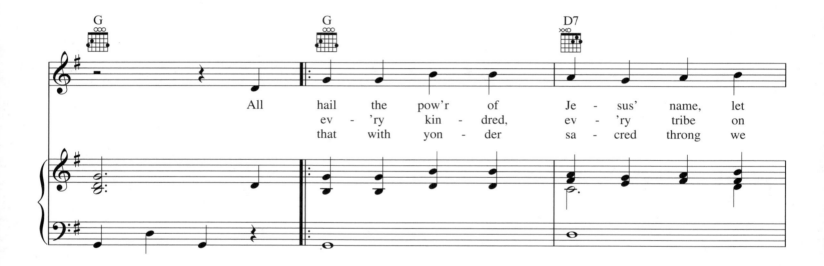

All hail the pow'r of Je - sus' name, let
ev - 'ry kin - dred, ev - 'ry tribe on
that with yon - der sa - cred throng we

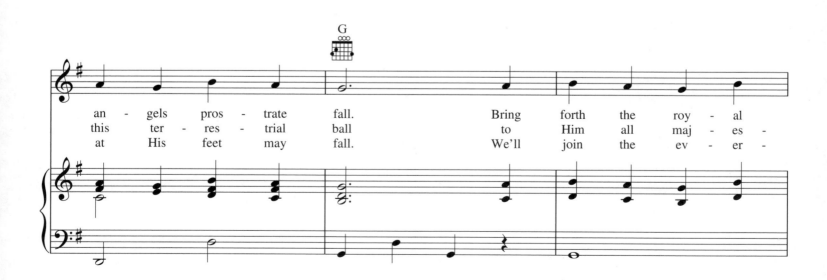

an - gels pros - trate fall. Bring forth the roy - al
this ter - res - trial ball to Him all maj - es -
at His feet may fall. We'll join the ev - er -

AWESOME GOD

Words and Music by
RICH MULLINS

Powerfully, in 2

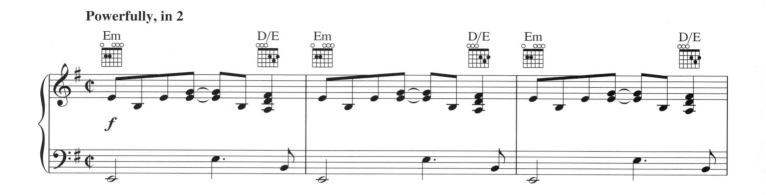

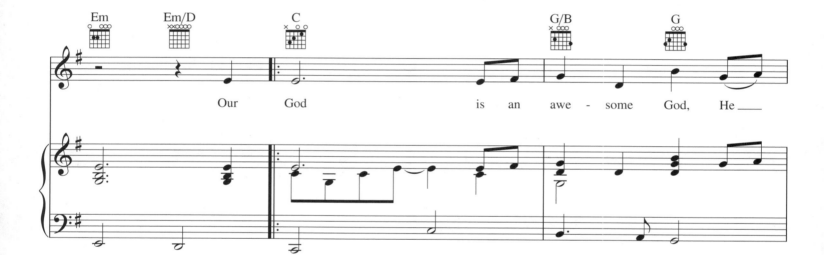

Our God is an awe- some God, He ___

reigns from ___ heav- en a - bove with ___ wis - dom, ___

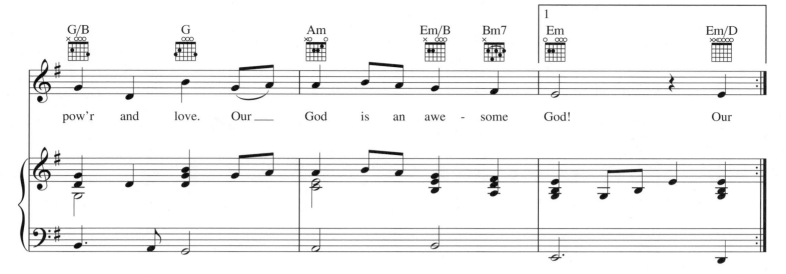

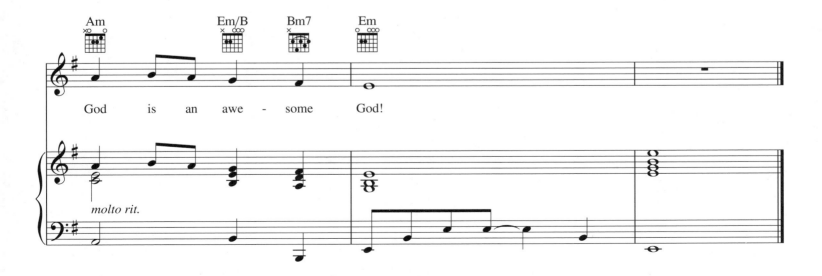

BE THOU MY VISION

Traditional Irish
Translated by MARY E. BYRNE

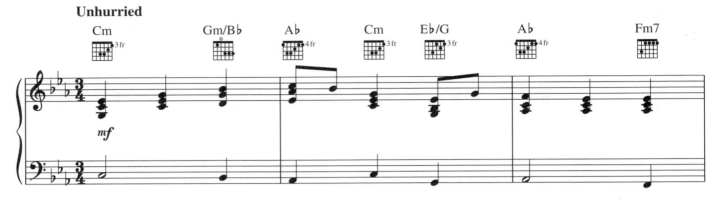

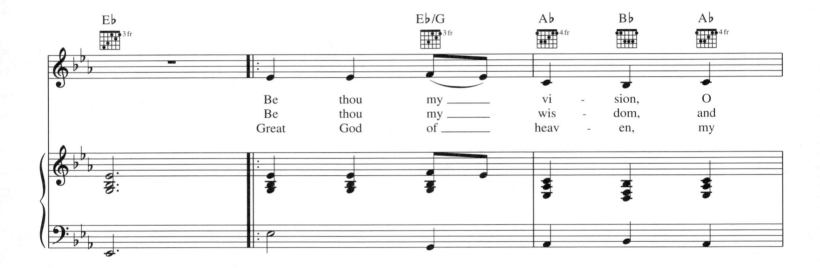

Be thou my _____ vi - sion, O
Be thou my _____ wis - dom, and
Great God of _____ heav - en, my

Lord of my heart; naught be all else to me,
thou my true word; I ev - er with thee and
vic - to - ry won, may I reach heav - en's joys,

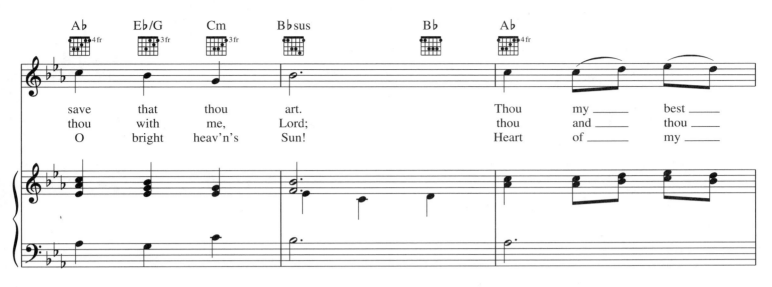

save   that   thou   art.   Thou   my _____   best _____
thou   with   me,   Lord;   thou   and _____   thou _____
O   bright heav'n's Sun!   Heart   of _____   my _____

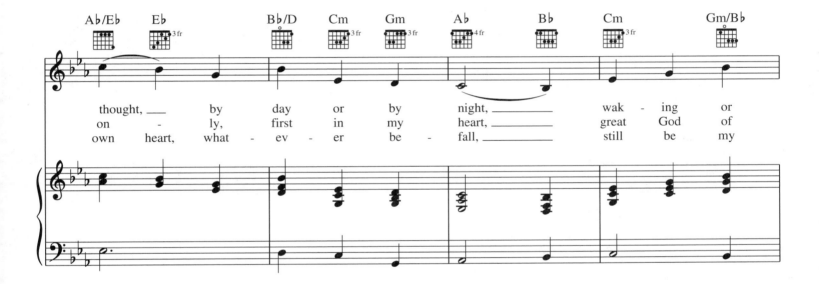

thought, ___   by   day   or   by   night, _____   wak - ing   or
on   -   ly,   day   first   in   my   heart, _____   great   God   of
own   heart,   what - ev -   er   be -   fall, _____   still   be   my

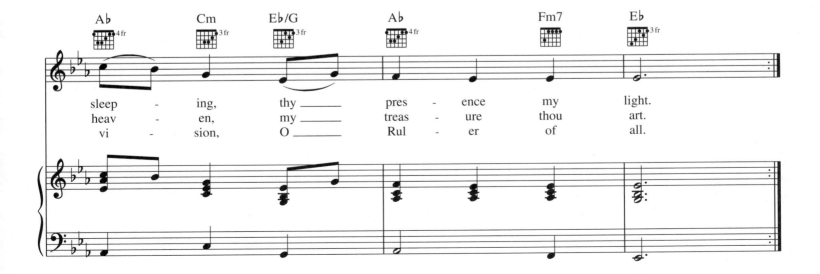

sleep - ing,   thy _____   pres - ence   my   light.
heav - en,   my _____   treas - ure   thou   art.
vi - sion,   O _____   Rul - er   of   all.

BLESS HIS HOLY NAME

Words and Music by
ANDRAÉ CROUCH

With a steady beat

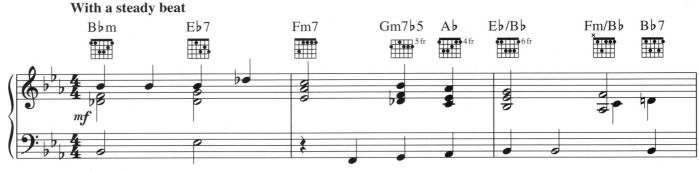

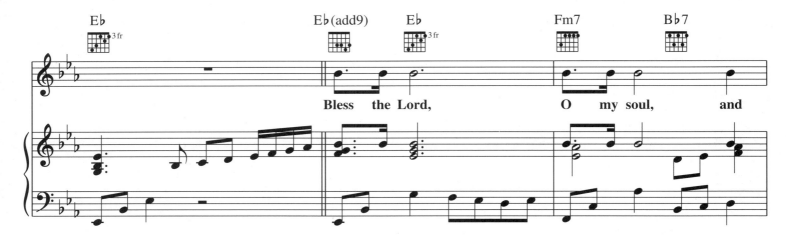

Bless the Lord, O my soul, and

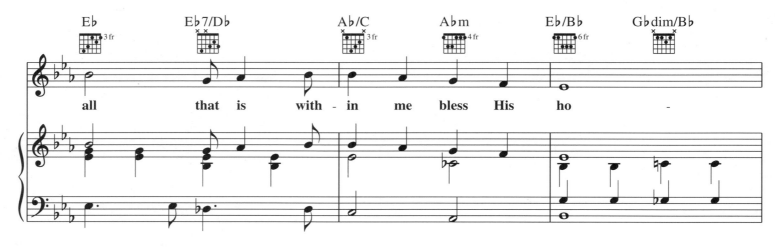

all that is with - in me bless His ho -

ly _____ Name. Bless the Lord,

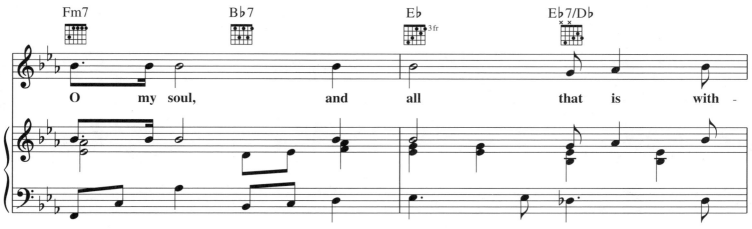

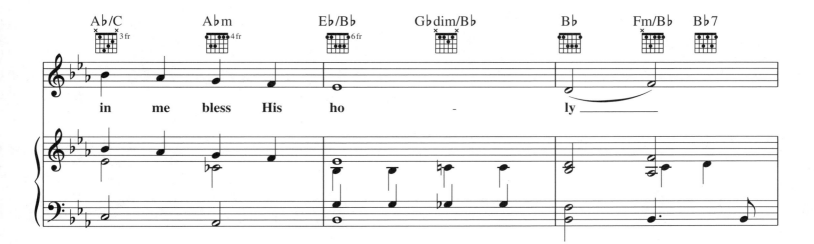

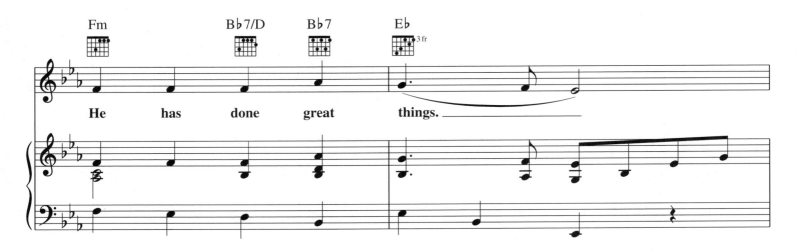

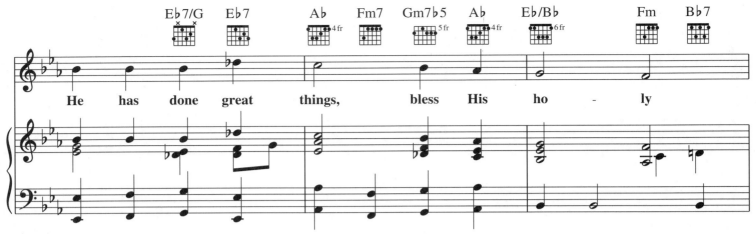

He has done great things, bless His ho - ly

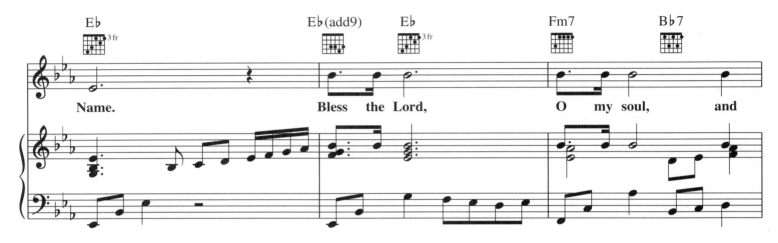

Name. Bless the Lord, O my soul, and

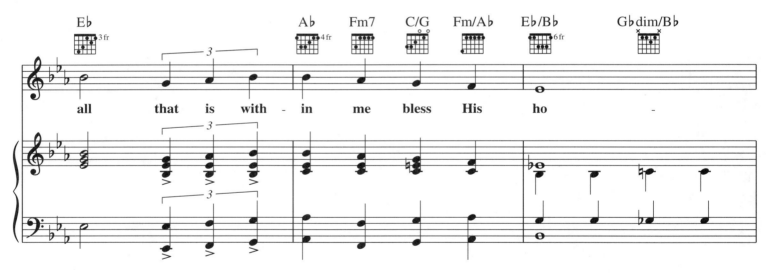

all that is with - in me bless His ho -

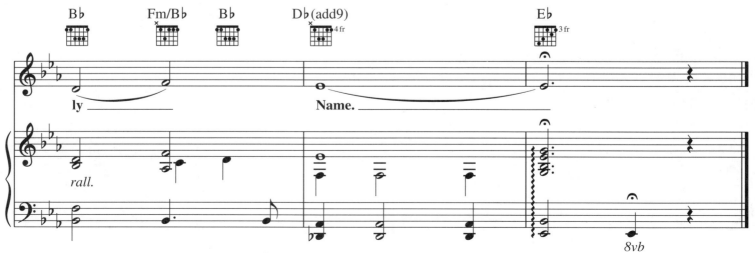

ly _____ Name. _____

rall.

8vb

GIVE THANKS

Words and Music by
HENRY SMITH

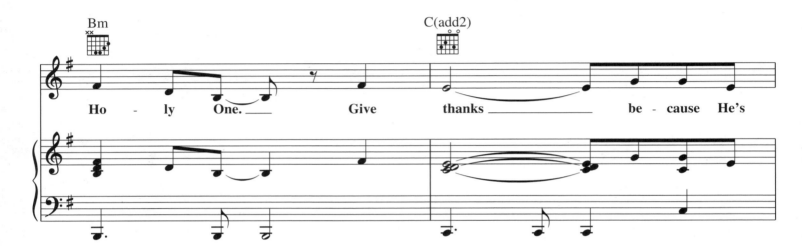

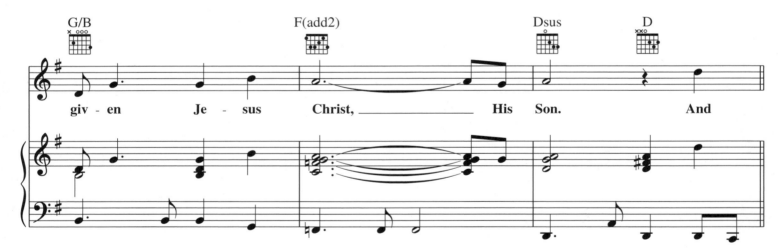

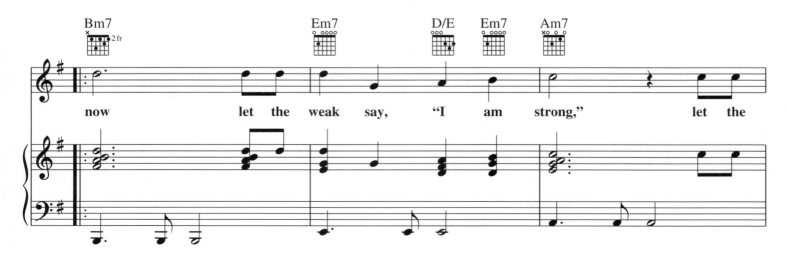

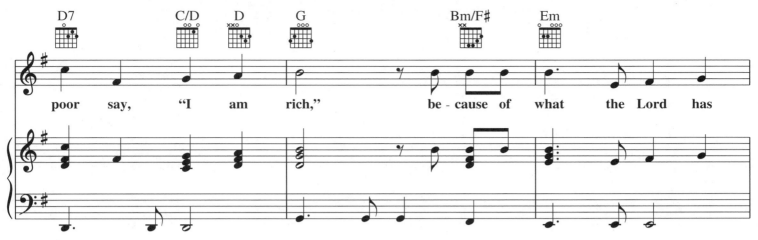

poor say, "I am rich," be - cause of what the Lord has

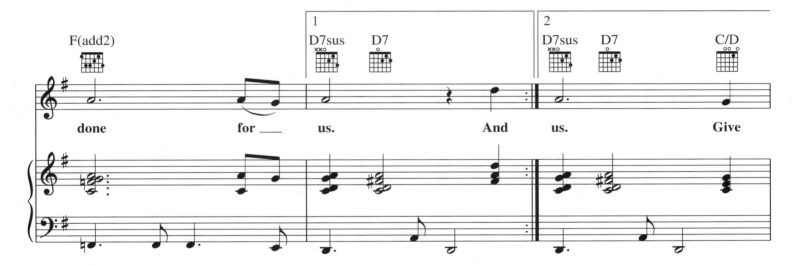

done for ___ us. And us. Give

thanks, _____ we give ___ thanks, _____

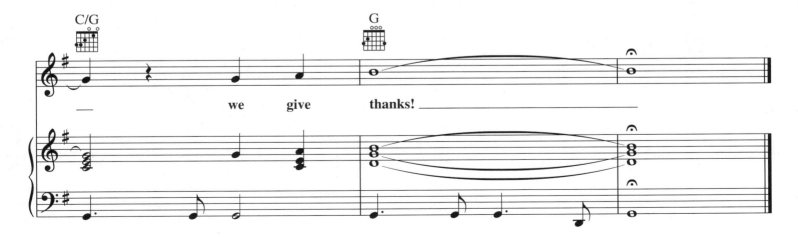

___ we give thanks! _____

BLESSED BE THE NAME

Words by WILLIAM H. CLARK (verses)
and RALPH E. HUDSON (refrain)
Traditional Music

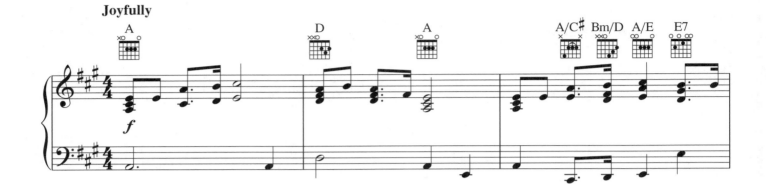

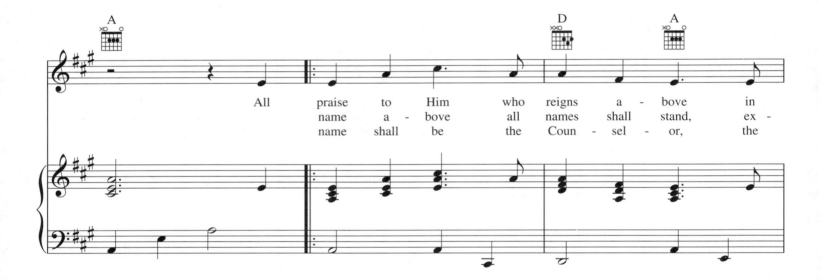

All praise to Him who reigns a - bove, in
name a - bove all names shall stand, ex -
name shall be the Coun - sel - or, the

maj - es - ty su - preme,   who gave His Son for
alt - ed more and more,   at God the Fa - ther's
might - y Prince of Peace,   of all earth's king - doms

BREATHE ON ME, BREATH OF GOD

Words by EDWIN HATCH
Music by ROBERT JACKSON

COME INTO HIS PRESENCE

Words and Music by
LYNN BAIRD

Brightly

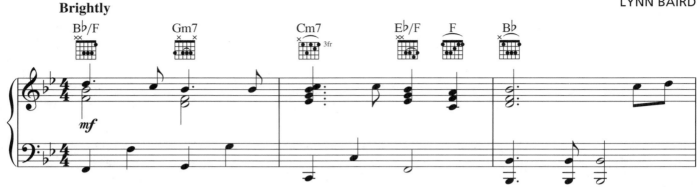

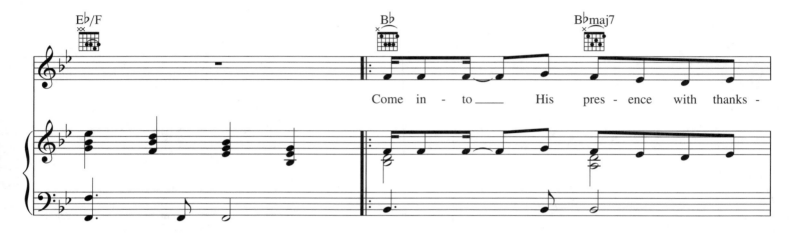

Come in-to ____ His pres-ence with thanks-

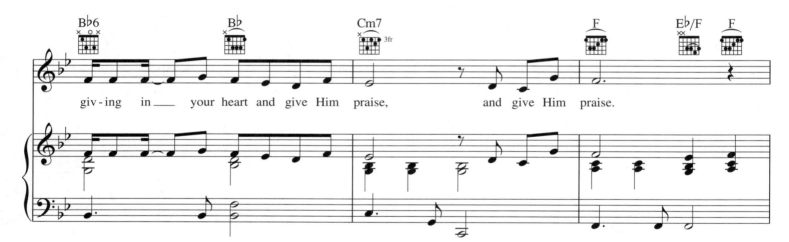

giv-ing in ____ your heart and give Him praise, and give Him praise.

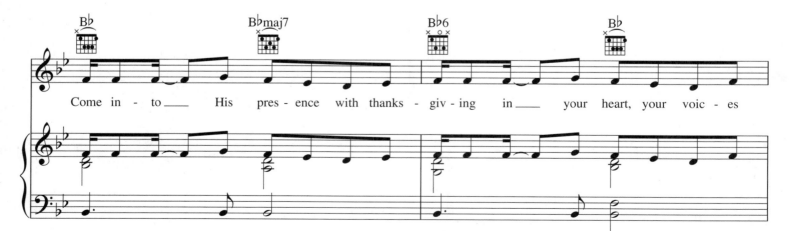

Come in-to ____ His pres-ence with thanks-giv-ing in ____ your heart, your voic-es

raise, your voic - es raise. Give glo - ry and

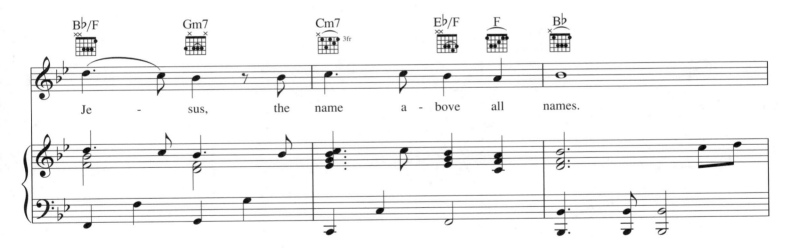

hon - or and pow - er un - to Him, _____

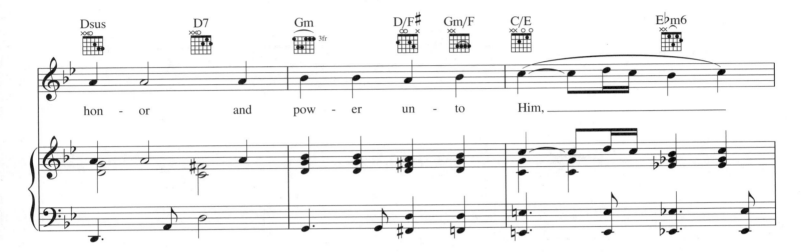

Je - sus, the name a - bove all names.

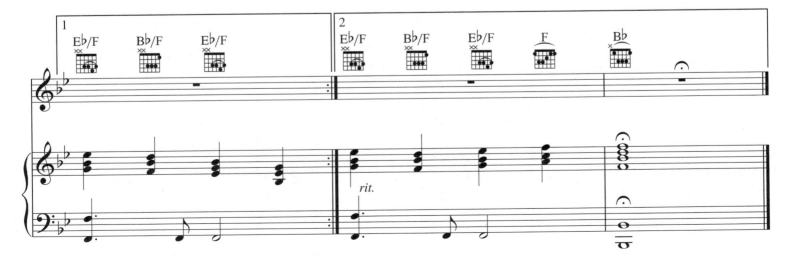

COME, NOW IS THE TIME TO WORSHIP

Words and Music by
BRIAN DOERKSEN

Driving Rock

Come, now is the time ___ to wor -

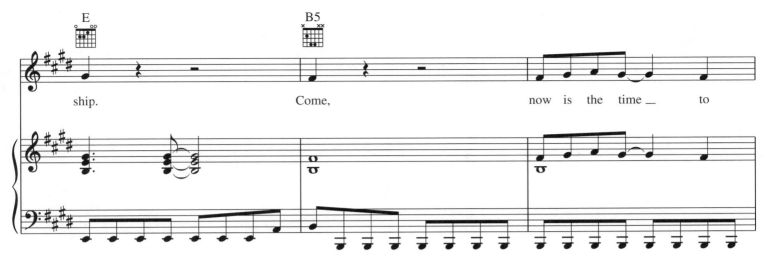

ship.   Come,   now is the time __ to

give   your _____ heart.   Come,

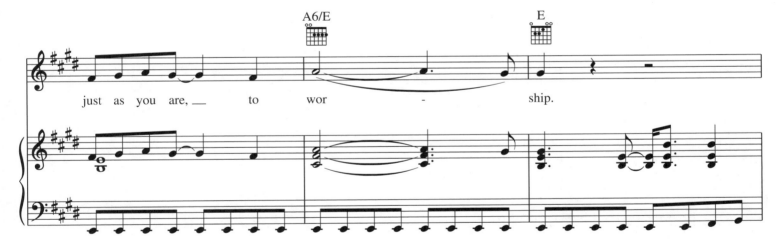

just as you are, __ to wor - ship.

Come,   just as you are, __ be - fore   your _____

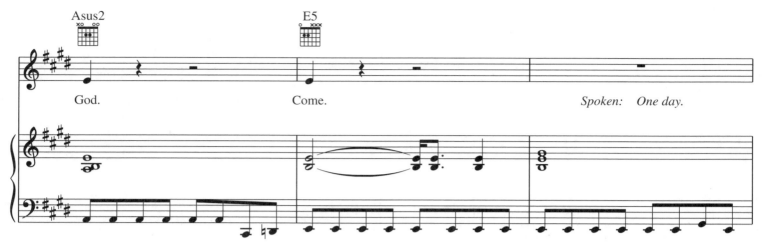

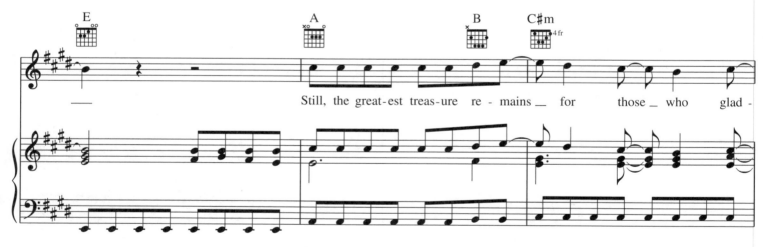

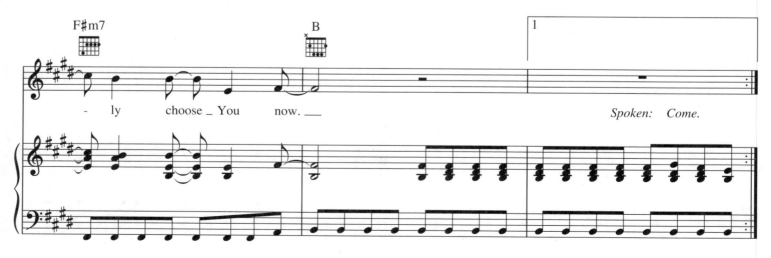

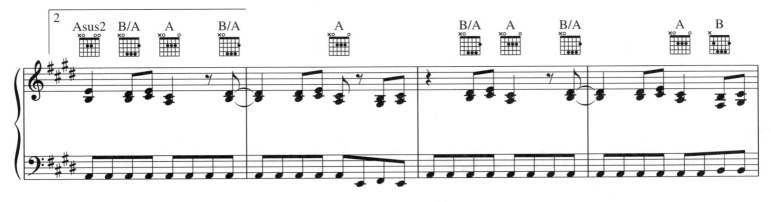

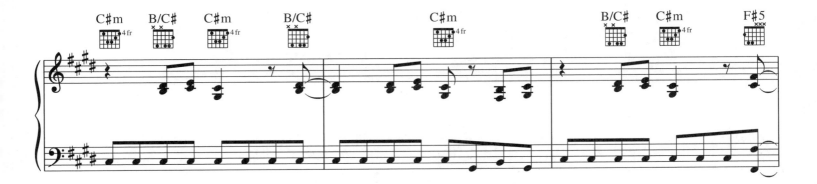

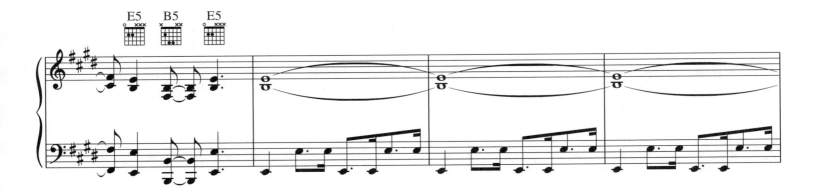

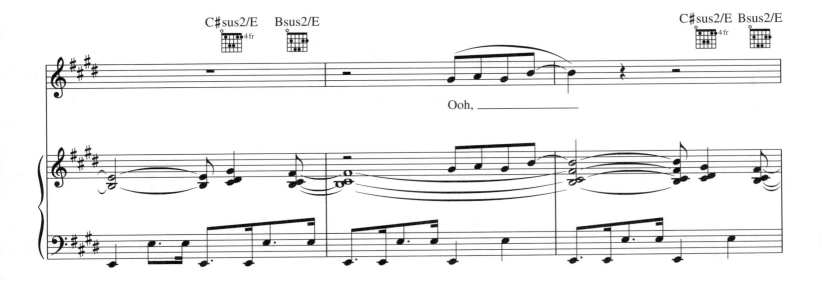

Ooh,

-ly choose _ You now. __ *Spoken: One day.* __

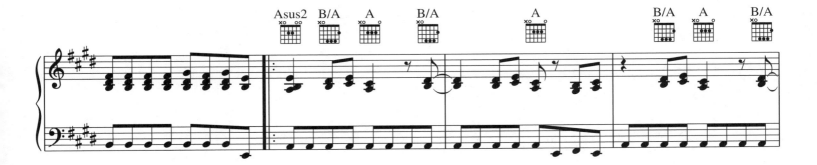

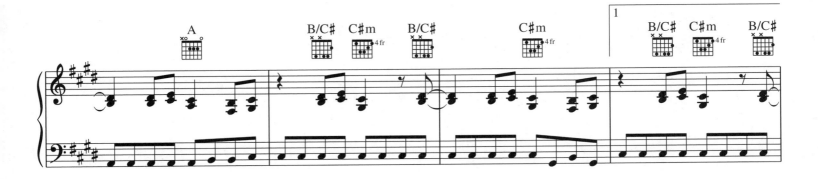

8vb

CROWN HIM WITH MANY CROWNS

Words by MATTHEW BRIDGES
and GODFREY THRING
Music by GEORGE JOB ELVEY

FAIREST LORD JESUS

Words from *Münster Gesangbuch*
Verse 4 by JOSEPH A. SEISS
Music from *Schlesische Volkslieder*

Fair - est Lord Je - sus, Rul - er of all
Fair are the mead - ows, Fair - er still the
Fair is the sun - shine, Fair - er still the
Beau - ti - ful Sav - ior! Lord _____ of the

na - ture, O Thou of God and _____
wood - lands, Robed in the bloom - ing _____
moon - light, And all the twin - kling _____
na - tions! Son of _____ God and _____

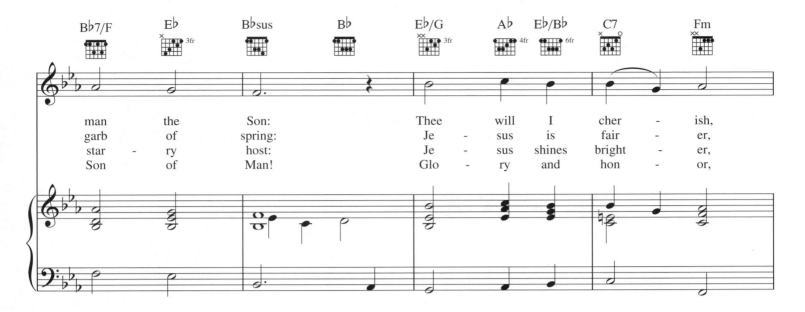

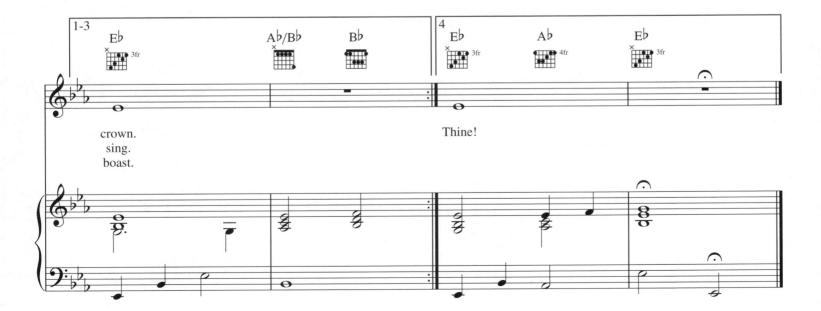

FOR THE BEAUTY OF THE EARTH

Words by FOLLIOT S. PIERPOINT
Music by CONRAD KOCHER

Gently, flowing

For the __ beau - ty of the earth, for the glo - ry

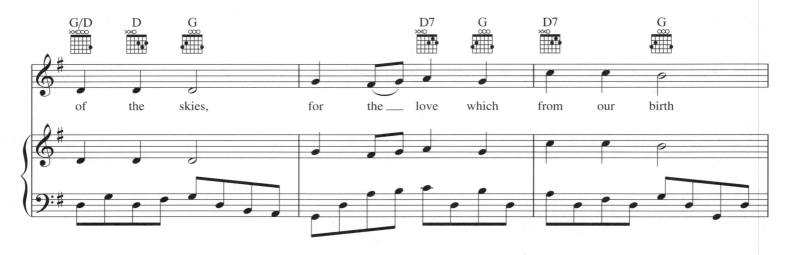

of the skies, for the __ love which from our birth

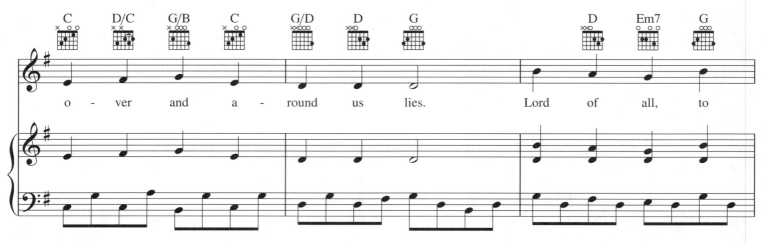

o - ver and a - round us lies. Lord of all, to

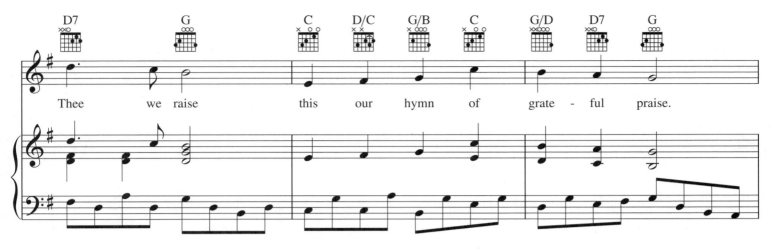

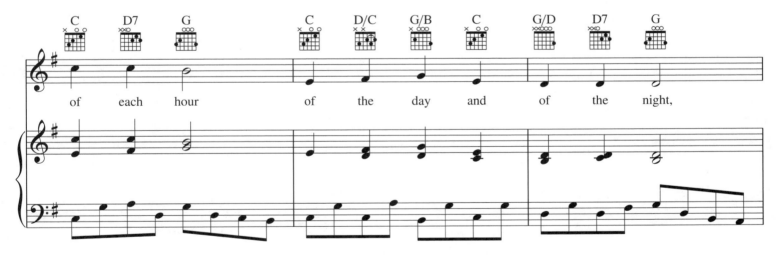

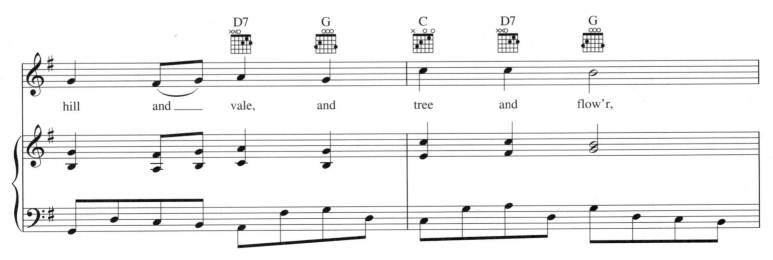

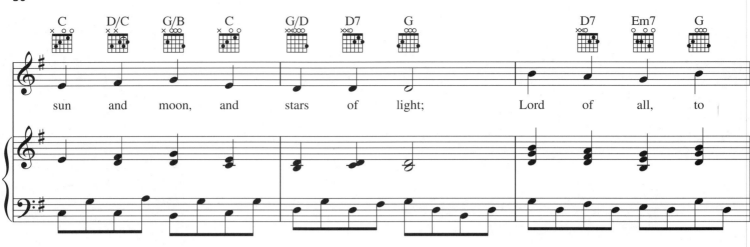

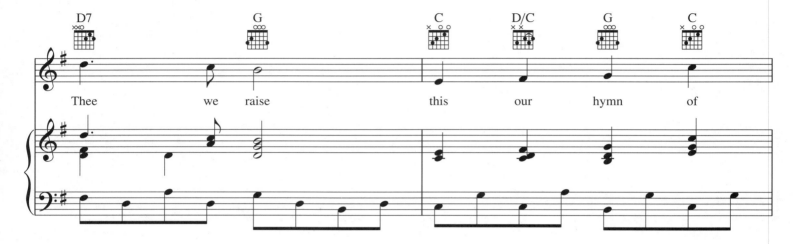

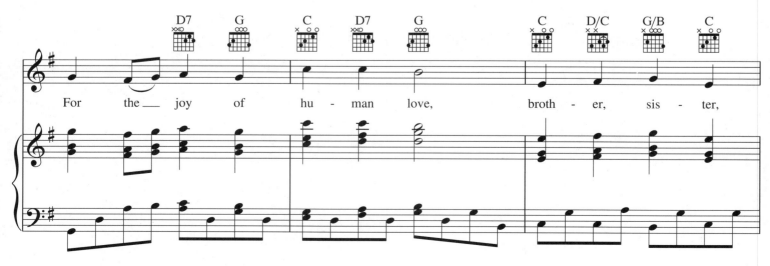

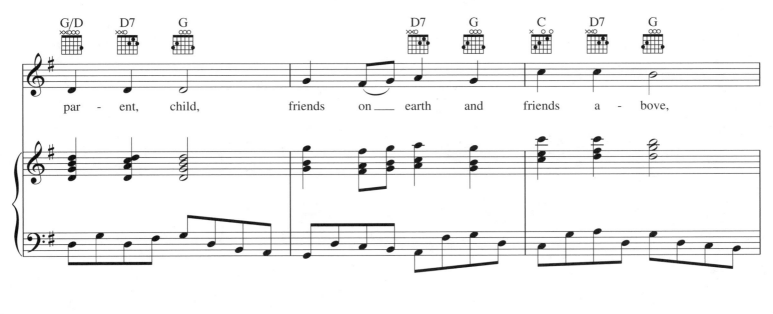

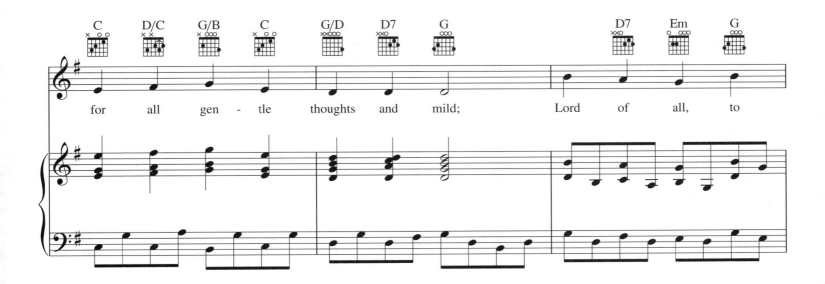

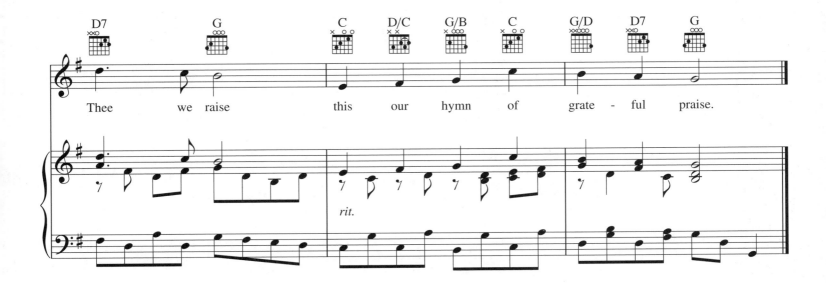

GREAT IS THE LORD

Words and Music by MICHAEL W. SMITH
and DEBORAH D. SMITH

GREAT IS THY FAITHFULNESS

Words by THOMAS O. CHISHOLM
Music by WILLIAM M. RUNYAN

With expression

Lyrics:

Great is Thy faith - ful - ness,
Sum - mer and win - ter and
Par - don for sin and a

O God my Fa - ther,
spring - time and har - vest,
peace that en - dur - eth,

There is no
Sun, moon and
Thine own dear

shad - ow of turn - ing with Thee.
stars in their cours - es a - bove
pres - ence to cheer and to guide,

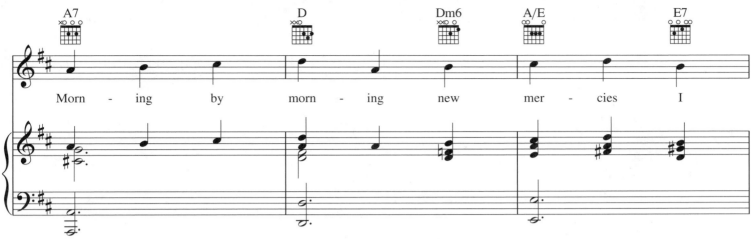

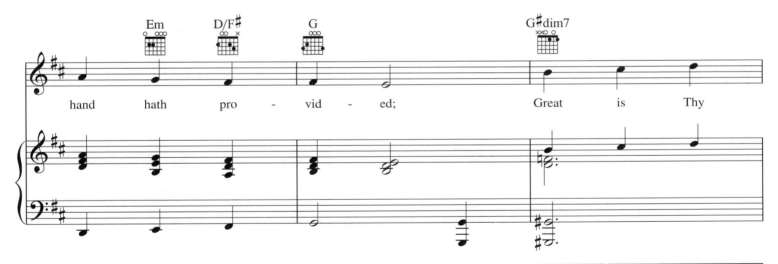

HAVE THINE OWN WAY, LORD

Words by ADELAIDE A. POLLARD
Music by GEORGE C. STEBBINS

Moderately slow

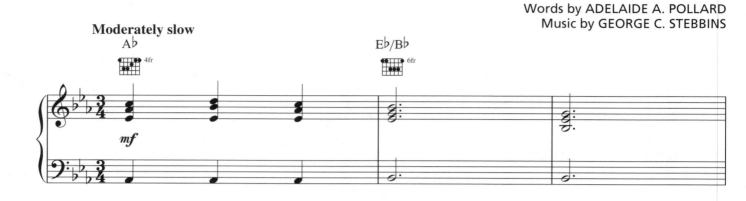

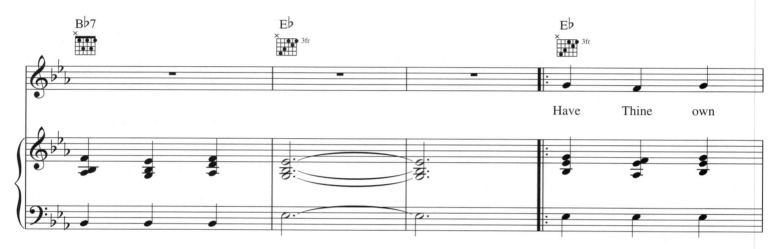

Have Thine own

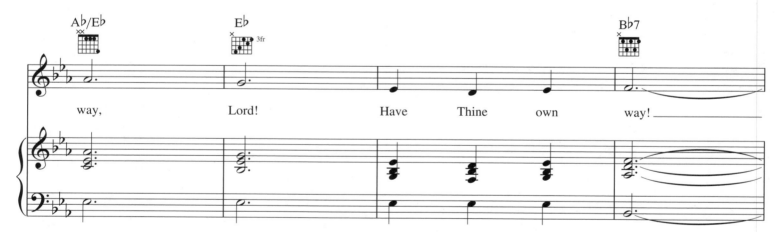

way, Lord! Have Thine own way! _____

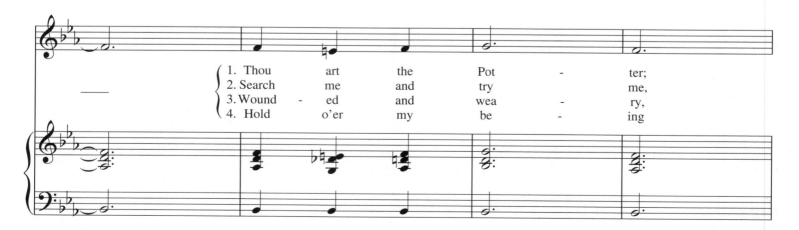

1. Thou art the Pot - ter;
2. Search me and try me,
3. Wound - ed and wea - ry,
4. Hold o'er my be - ing

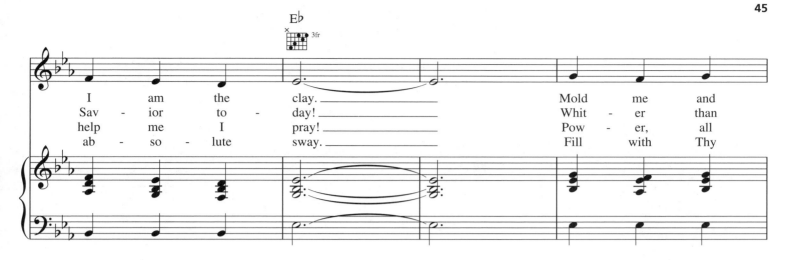

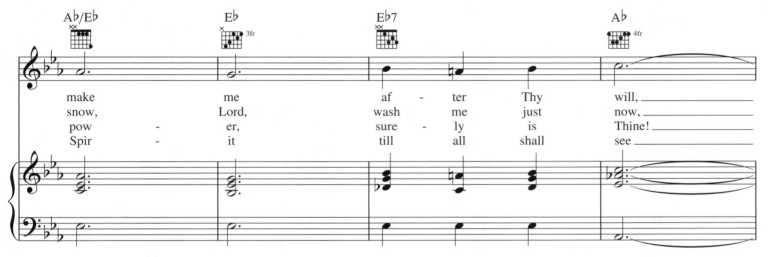

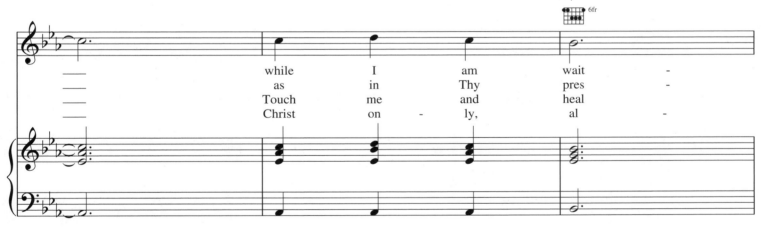

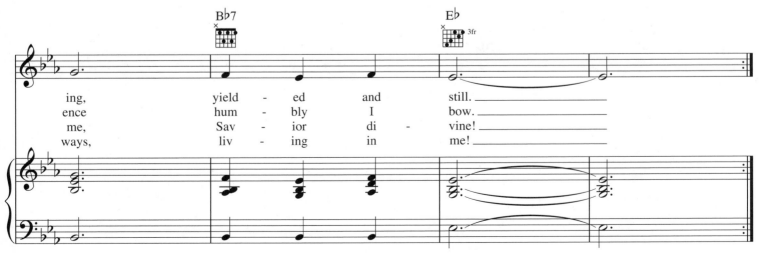

HE IS EXALTED

Words and Music by
TWILA PARIS

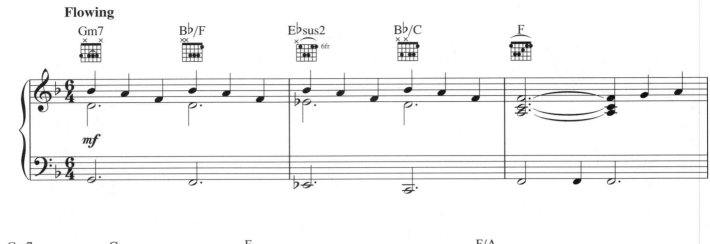

He is ex-alt-ed, the King is ex-alt-ed on ___

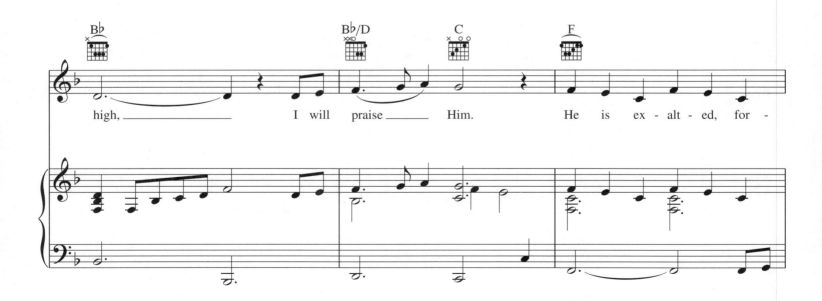

high, ___ I will praise ___ Him. He is ex-alt-ed, for-

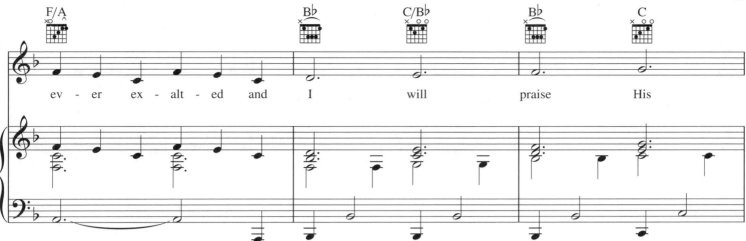

ev - er ex - alt - ed and I will praise His

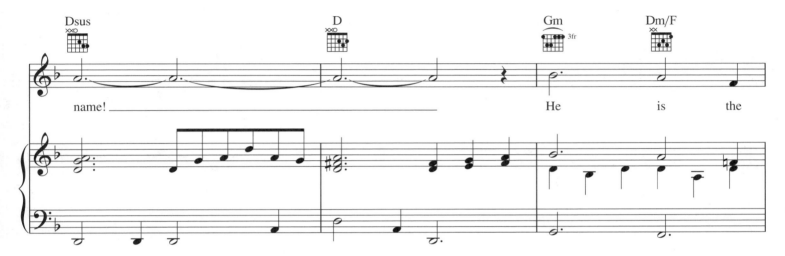

name! _____ He is the

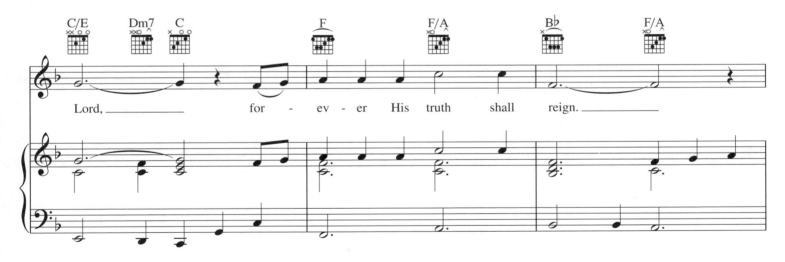

Lord, _____ for - ev - er His truth shall reign. _____

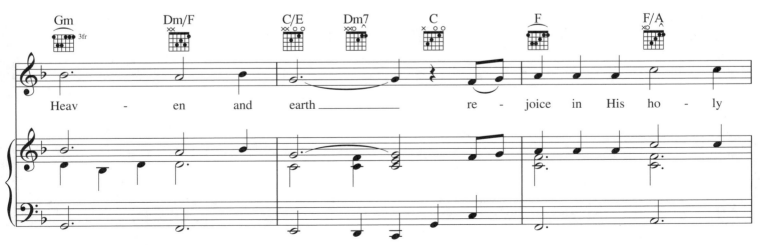

Heav - en and earth _____ re - joice in His ho - ly

HERE I AM TO WORSHIP

Words and Music by
TIM HUGHES

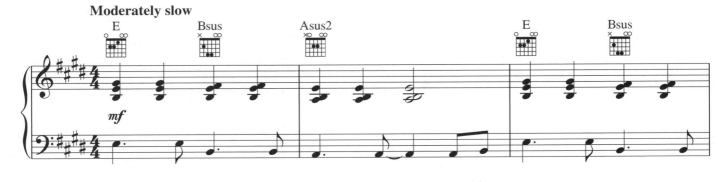

Here I am to wor - ship, here I am to bow down, here I am to

say that You're my God. ___ You're al - to - geth - er love - ly, al - to - geth - er

wor - thy, al - to - geth - er won - der - ful to me. ___

To Coda ⊕

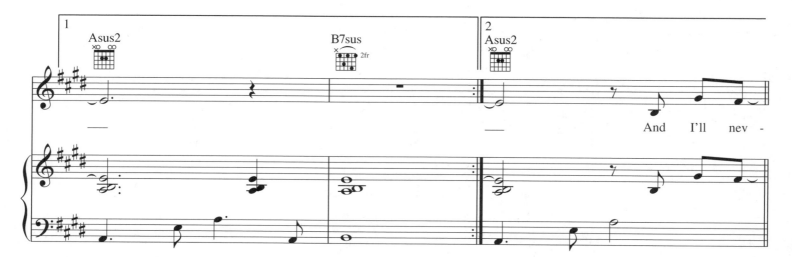

___ ___ And I'll nev -

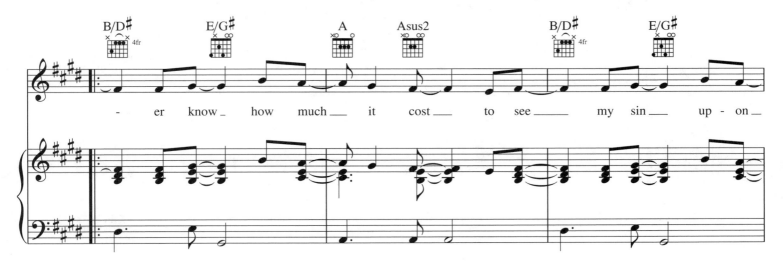

-er know_ how much_ it cost_ to see_ my sin_ up - on_

1 ___ that cross._ And I'll nev - ___ that cross._

2 ___ that cross._ **D.S. al Coda**

Here I am to

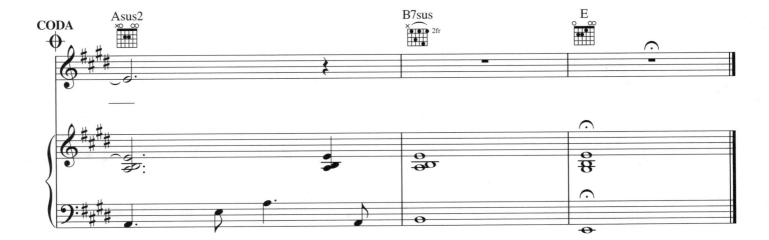

CODA

HIS NAME IS WONDERFUL

Words and Music by
AUDREY MIEIR

His name is Won-der-ful, His name is Won-der-ful, His name is

Won-der-ful, Je-sus, my Lord; He is the might-y King,

Mas-ter of ev-'ry-thing, His name is Won-der-ful, Je-sus, my

Lord. He's the great Shep - herd, the Rock of all

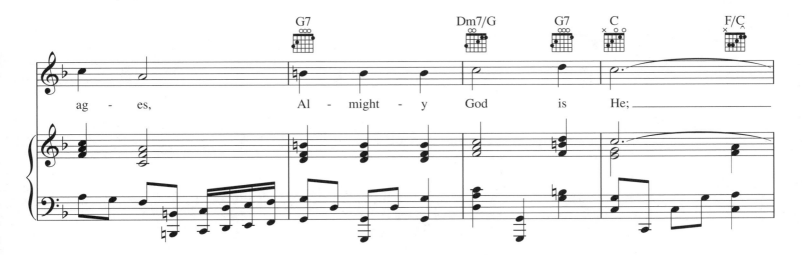

ag - es, Al - might - y God is He; _____

_____ Bow down be - fore Him, Love and a - dore Him,

His name is Won - der - ful, Je - sus my Lord.

HOLY, HOLY, HOLY

Text by REGINALD HEBER
Music by JOHN B. DYKES

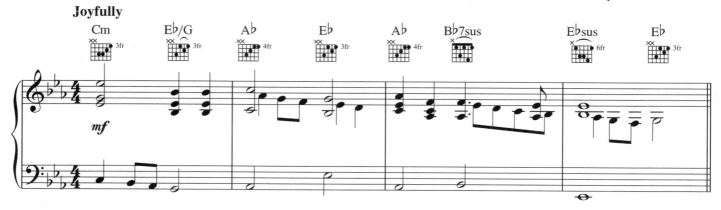

Ho - ly, ho - ly, ho - ly! Lord God Al -
Ho - ly, ho - ly, ho - ly! All the saints a -

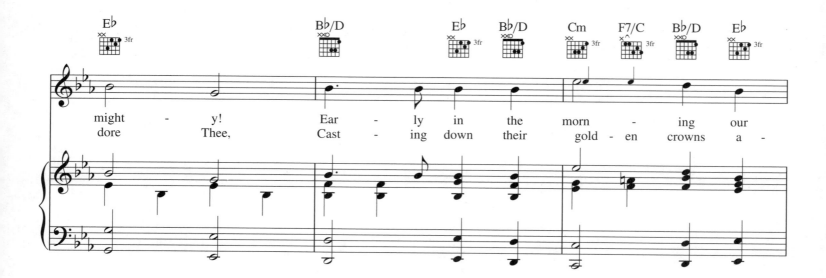

might - y! Ear - ly in the morn - ing our
dore Thee, Cast - ing down their gold - en crowns a -

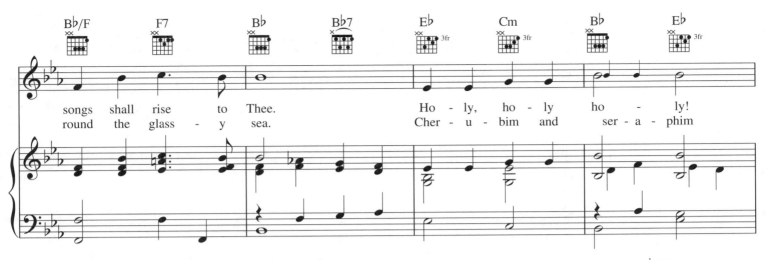

songs shall rise to Thee. Ho — ly, ho — ly ho — ly!
round the glass — y sea. Cher — u — bim and ser — a — phim

Mer — ci — ful and might — y! God in three
fall — ing down be — fore Thee, Which wert, and

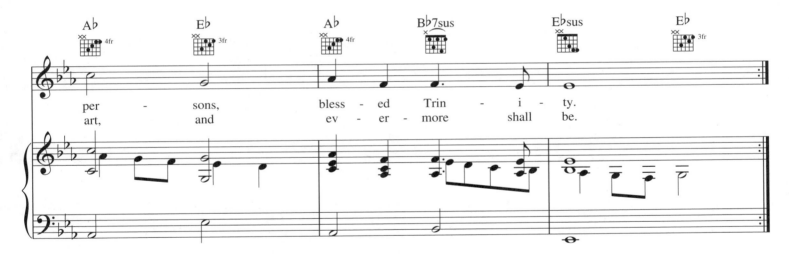

per — sons, bless — ed Trin — i — ty.
art, and ev — er — more shall be.

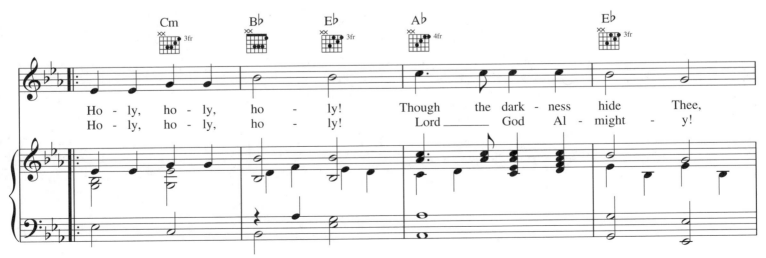

Ho — ly, ho — ly, ho — ly! Though the dark — ness hide Thee,
Ho — ly, ho — ly, ho — ly! Lord _____ God Al — might — y!

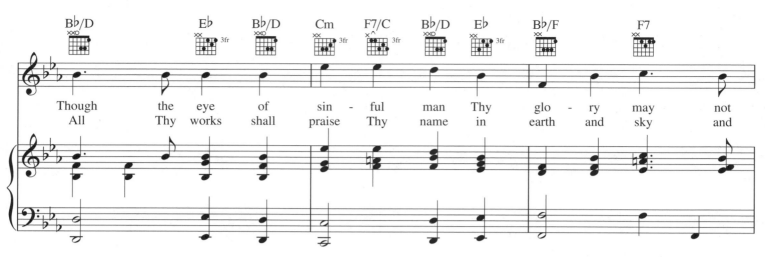

Though the eye of sin - ful man Thy glo - ry may not
All Thy works shall praise Thy name in earth and sky and

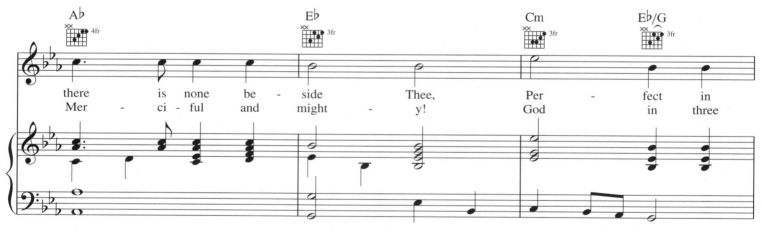

see. On - ly Thou art ho - ly;
sea. Ho - ly, ho - ly, ho - ly!

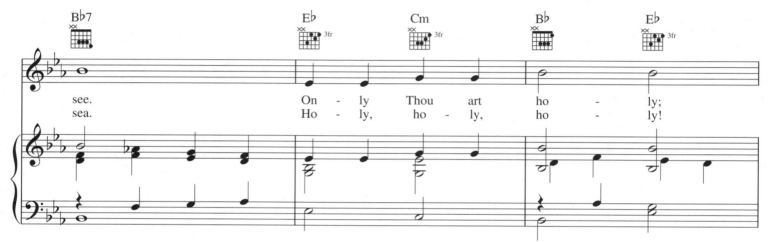

there is none be - side Thee, Per - fect in
Mer - ci - ful and might - y! God in three

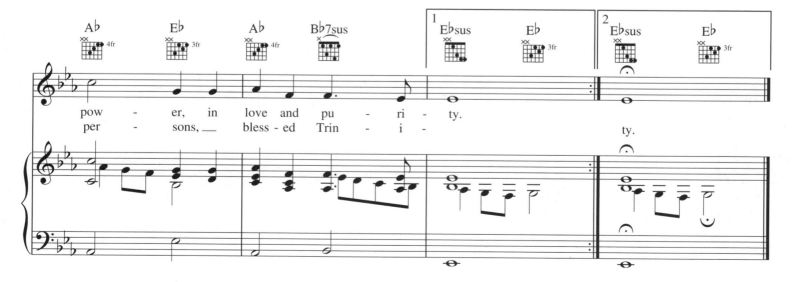

pow - er, in love and pu - ri - ty.
per - sons, __ bless - ed Trin - i - ty.

JESUS, NAME ABOVE ALL NAMES

Words and Music by
NAIDA HEARN

man - u - el, _____ God ___ is with us, _____

_____ bless - ed Re - deem - er, _____ liv - ing

Word.

Word.

Je - sus, _____ name a - bove all names, _____

beau - ti - ful Sav - ior, _____ glo - ri - ous

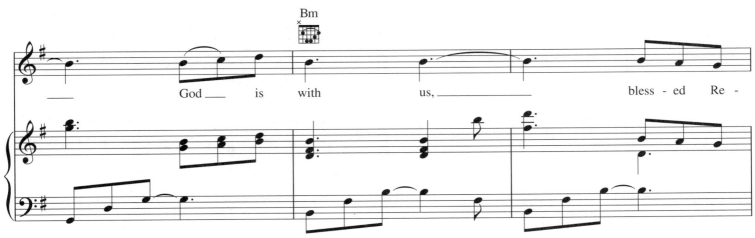

Lord. _____ Em - man - u - el, _____

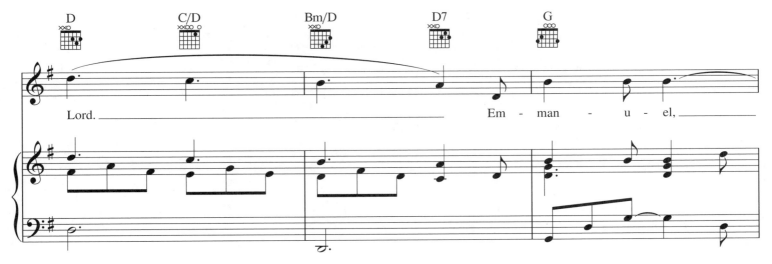

God ___ is with us, _____ bless - ed Re -

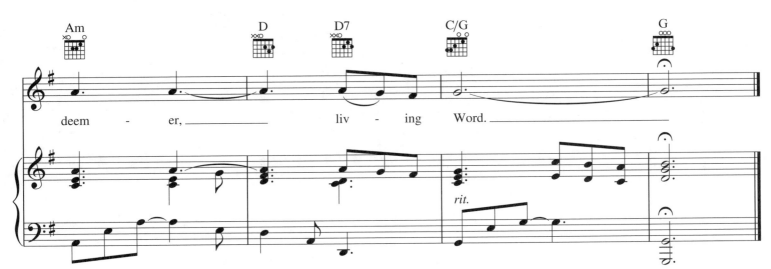

deem - er, _____ liv - ing Word. _____

HOW GREAT THOU ART

Words and Music by
STUART K. HINE

1. O Lord, my God! When I in awe-some won-der _____ con-sid-er
2. woods and for-est glades I wan-der _____ and hear the
3.,4. *(See additional verses)*

all the worlds Thy hands have made, _____ I see the stars, I hear the roll-ing
birds sing sweet-ly in the trees; _____ When I look down from loft-y moun-tain

thun-der, _____ Thy pow'r through-out the u-ni-verse dis-played, _____
gran-deur _____ and hear the brook and feel the gen-tle breeze; _____ } Then sings my

Additional Verses

3. And when I think that God, His Son not sparing,
Sent Him to die, I scarce can take it in;
That on the cross, my burden gladly bearing,
He bled and died to take away my sin.

4. When Christ shall come with shout of acclamation
And take me home, what joy shall fill my heart!
Then I shall bow in humble adoration
And there proclaim: My God, How great Thou art!

HOW MAJESTIC IS YOUR NAME

Words and Music by
MICHAEL W. SMITH

Majestically

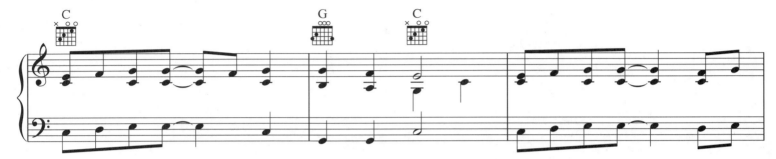

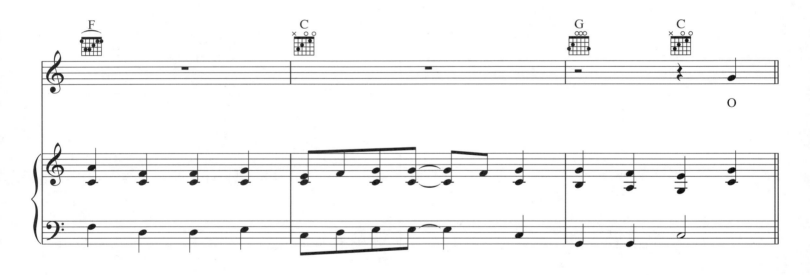

Lord, __ our Lord, __ how ma-jes-tic is Your name __ in all _____ the ___

earth. O Lord, __ our Lord, __ how ma - jes - tic is Your

name __ in all _____ the __ earth. O __ Lord, _____

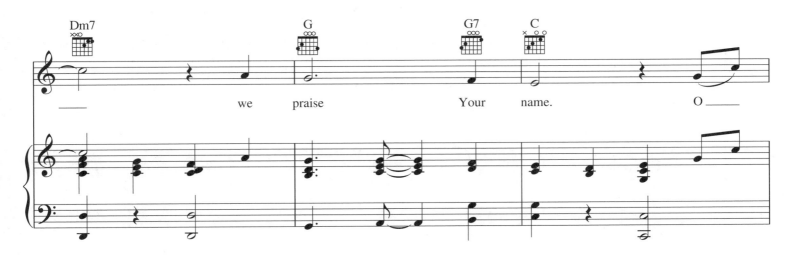

__ we praise Your name. O __

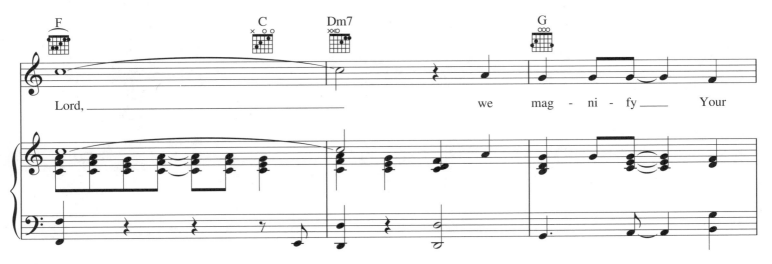

Lord, _____ we mag - ni - fy __ Your

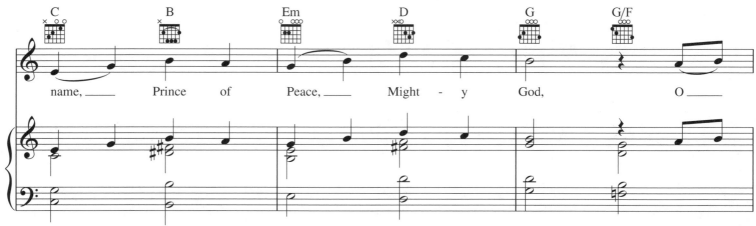

name, _____ Prince of Peace, _____ Might - y God, O _____

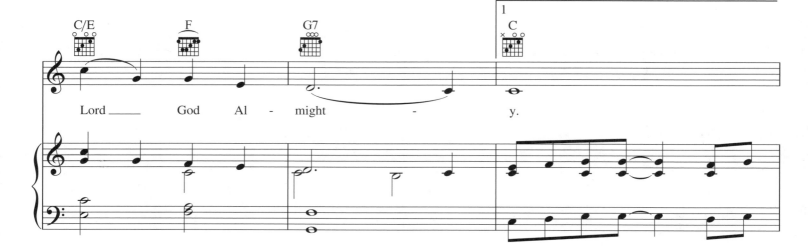

Lord _____ God Al - might - y.

O

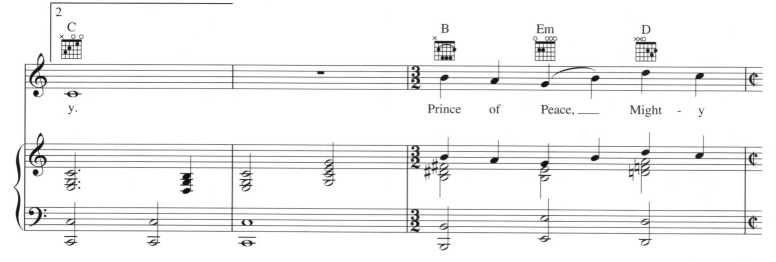

y. Prince of Peace, _____ Might - y

God, O _____ Lord _____ God Al - might -

y. _____

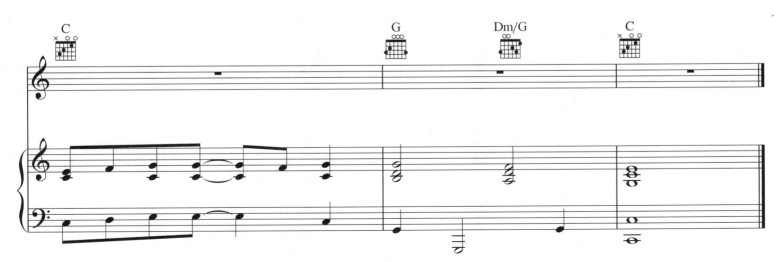

I SING PRAISES

Words and Music by
TERRY MacALMON

I sing prais-es to Your name, O ____ Lord, prais-es to Your
name, O ____ Lord, glo-ry to Your

name, O ____ Lord, for Your name is great and
name, O ____ Lord, for Your name is great and

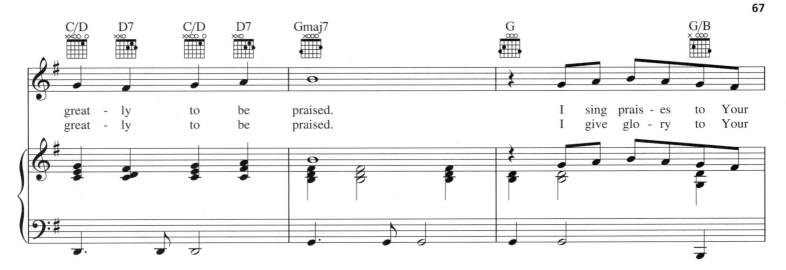

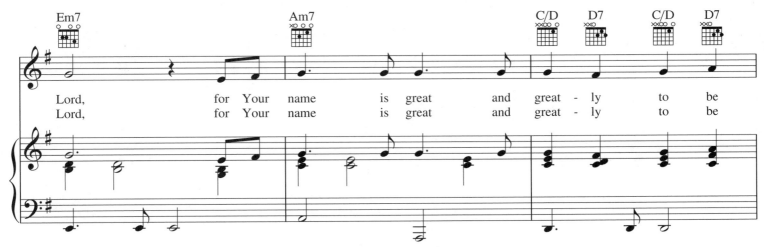

I SING THE MIGHTY POWER OF GOD

Words by ISAAC WATTS
Music from *Gesangbuch der Herzogl*

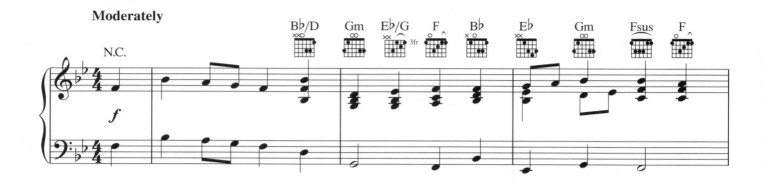

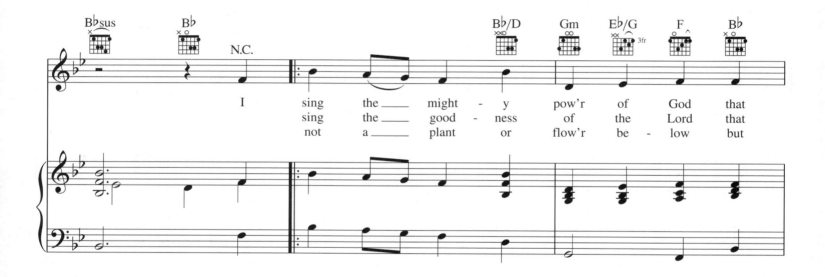

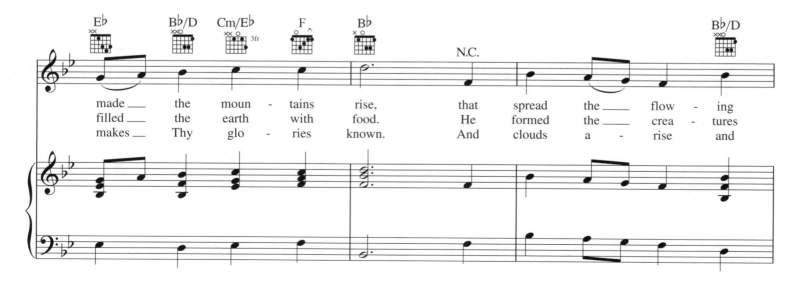

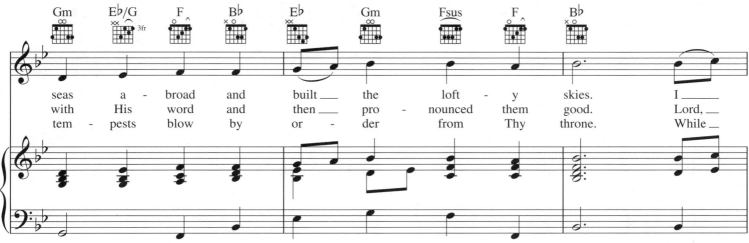

seas a - broad and built __ the loft - y skies. I _____
with His word and then __ pro - nounced them good. Lord, __
tem - pests blow by or - der from Thy throne. While __

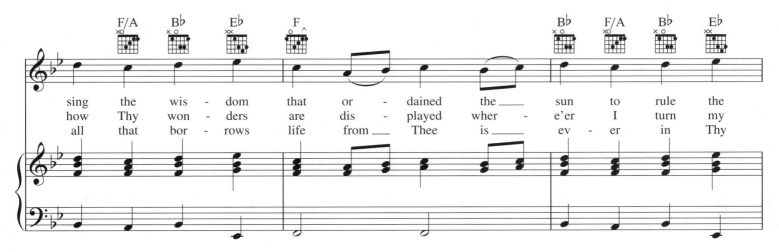

sing the wis - dom that or - dained the __ sun to rule the
how Thy won - ders are dis - played wher - e'er I turn my
all that bor - rows life from __ Thee is __ ev - er in Thy

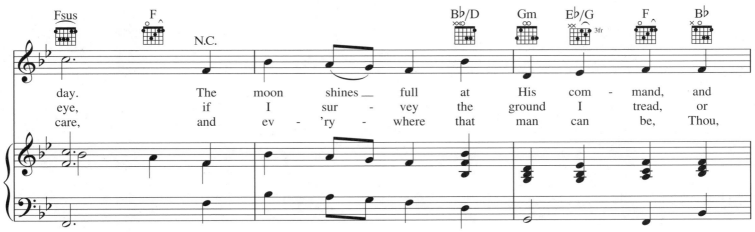

day. The moon shines __ full at His com - mand, and
eye, if I sur - vey the His ground I tread, or
care, and ev - 'ry - where that man can be, Thou,

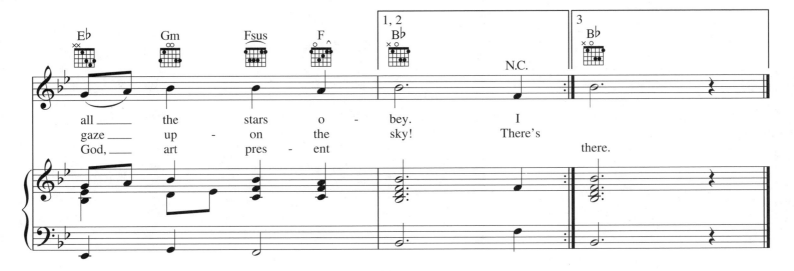

all _____ the stars o - bey. I
gaze ___ up - on the sky! There's
God, ___ art pres - ent there.

I WORSHIP YOU, ALMIGHTY GOD

Words and Music by
SONDRA CORBETT-WOOD

Moderately, not too slow

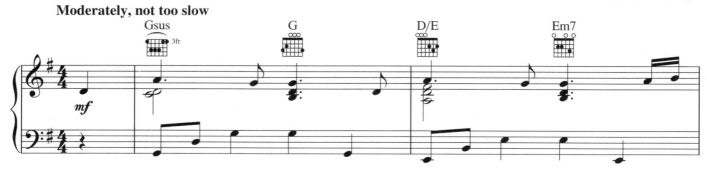

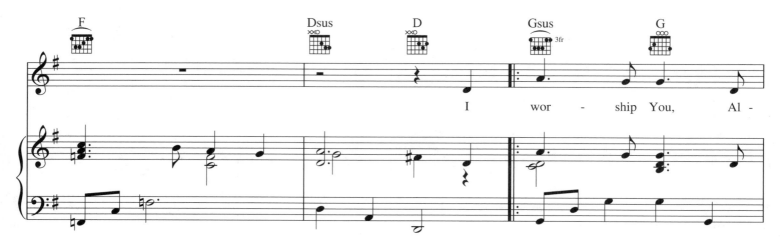

I   wor - ship You,   Al -

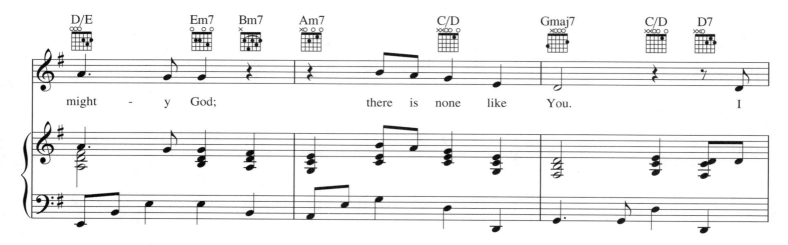

might - y God;   there is none   like   You.   I

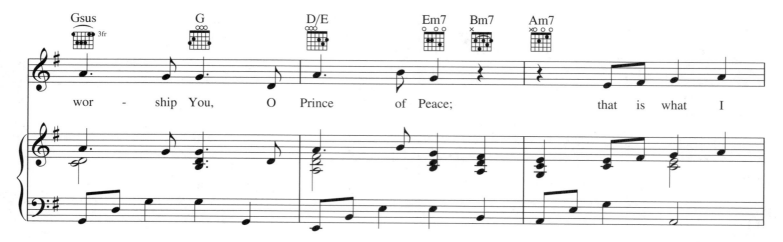

wor - ship You,   O   Prince   of Peace;   that is what I

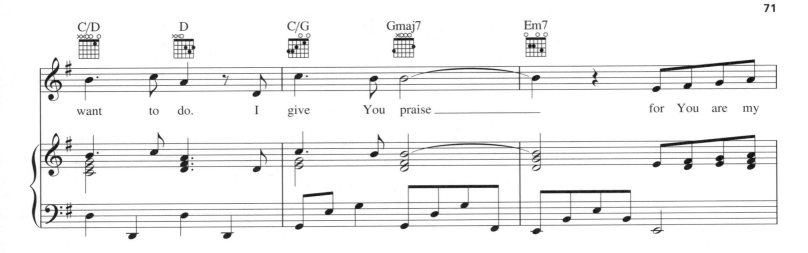

want to do. I give You praise _____ for You are my

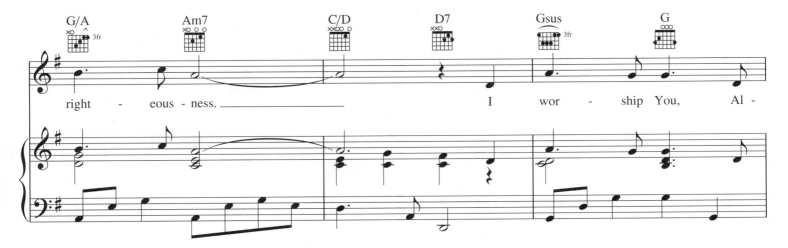

right - eous - ness. _____ I wor - ship You, Al -

might - y God; there is none like You. I

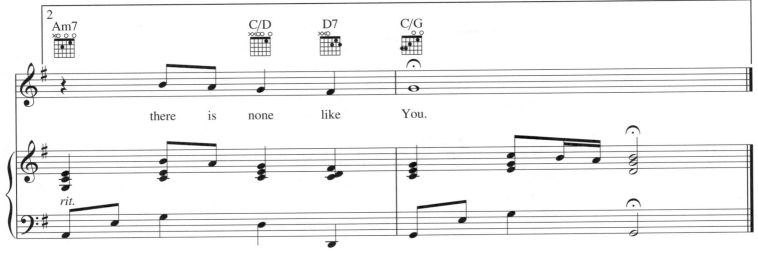

there is none like You.

LORD, I LIFT YOUR NAME ON HIGH

Words and Music by
RICK FOUNDS

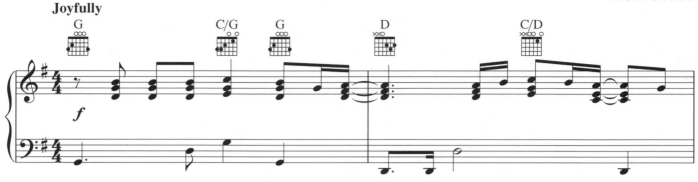

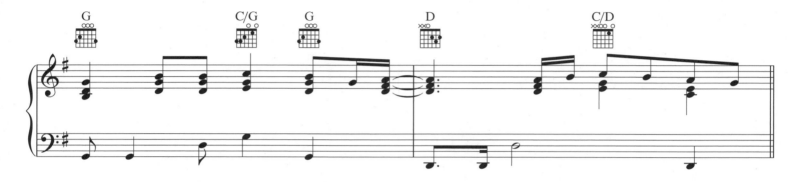

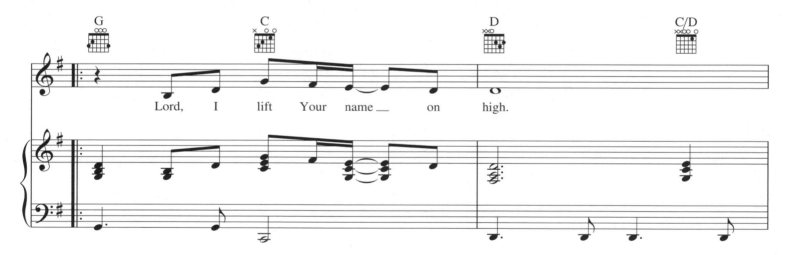

Lord, I lift Your name __ on high.

Lord, I love to sing __ Your prais - es.

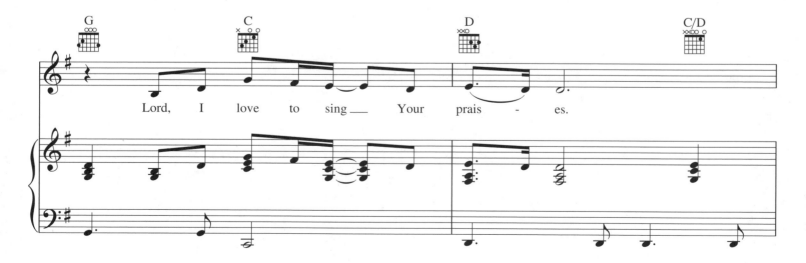

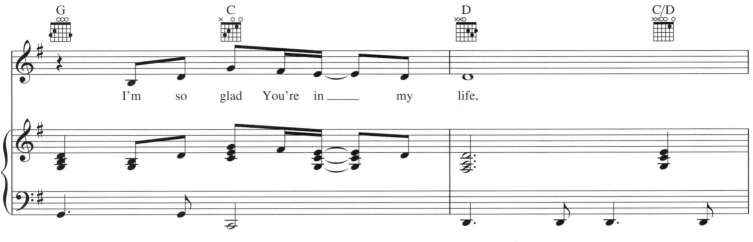

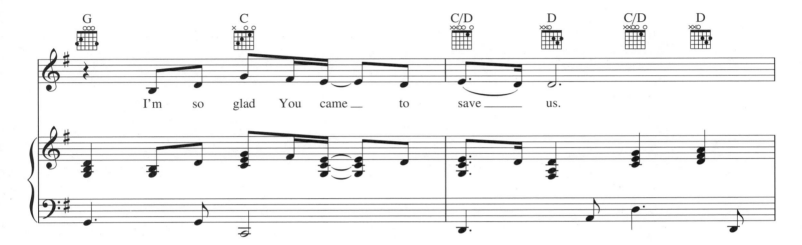

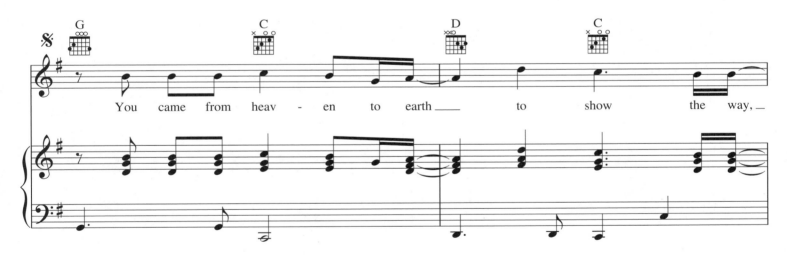

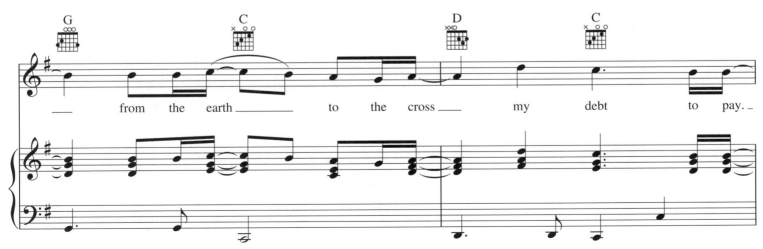

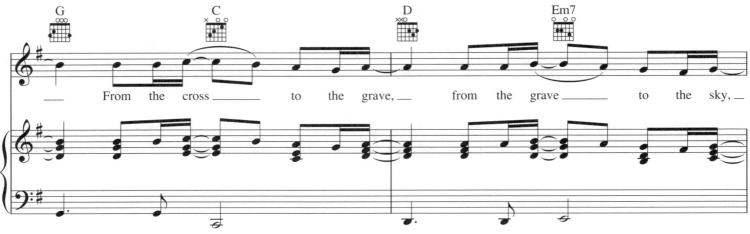

From the cross _____ to the grave, __ from the grave _____ to the sky, __

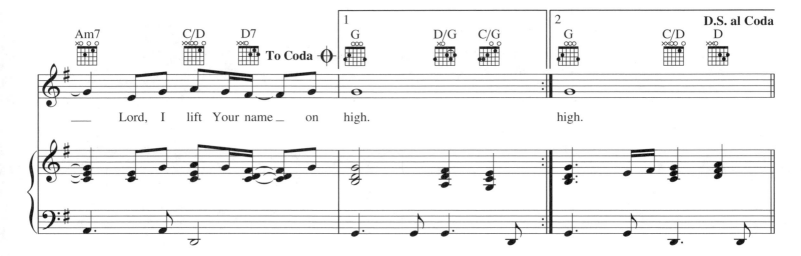

Lord, I lift Your name __ on high.   high.

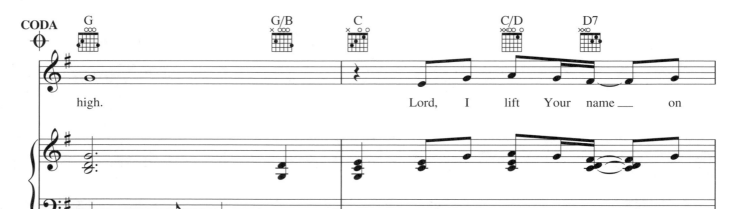

CODA

high.   Lord, I lift Your name ____ on

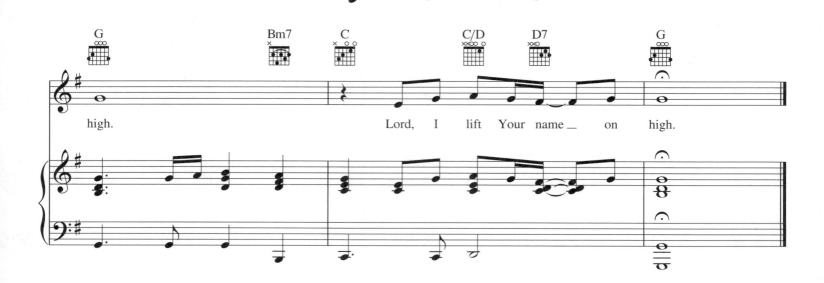

high.   Lord, I lift Your name __ on high.

MY LIFE IS IN YOU, LORD

Words and Music by
DANIEL GARDNER

Driving

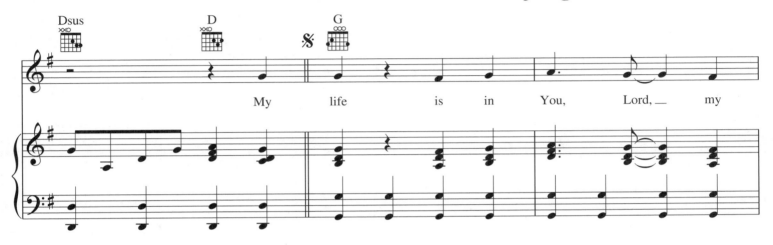

My life is in You, Lord, ___ my

strength is in You, Lord, ___ my hope is in

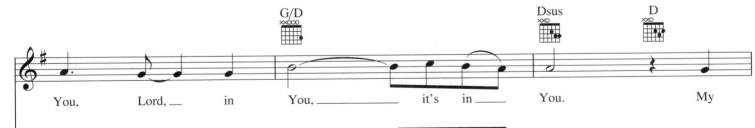

You, Lord, ___ in You, _____ it's in ___ You. My

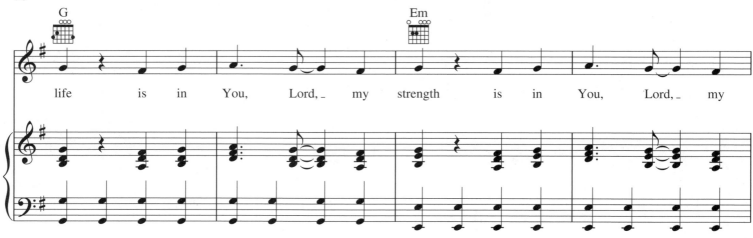

life is in You, Lord, _ my strength is in You, Lord, _ my

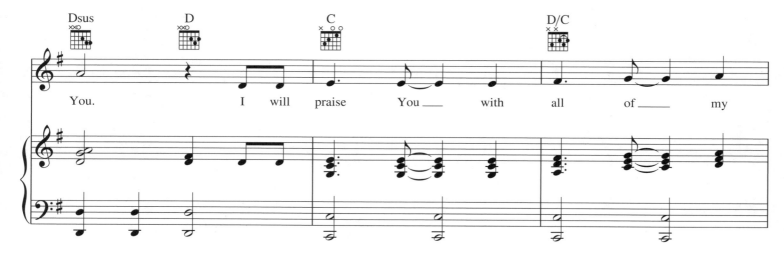

hope is in You, Lord, _ in You, _____ it's in _____

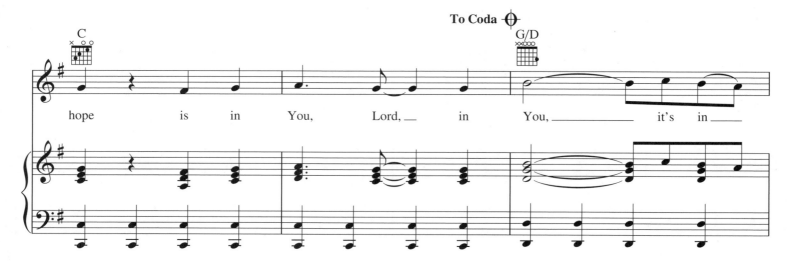

You. I will praise You __ with all of _____ my

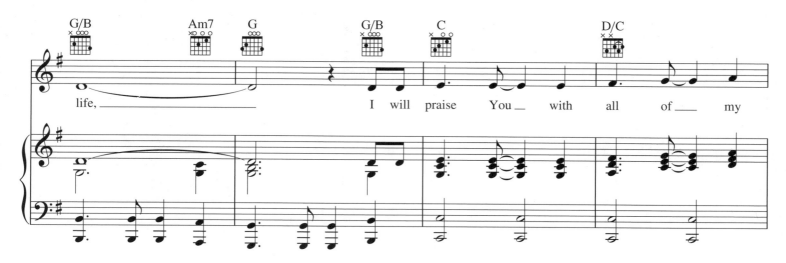

life, _____ I will praise You __ with all of ___ my

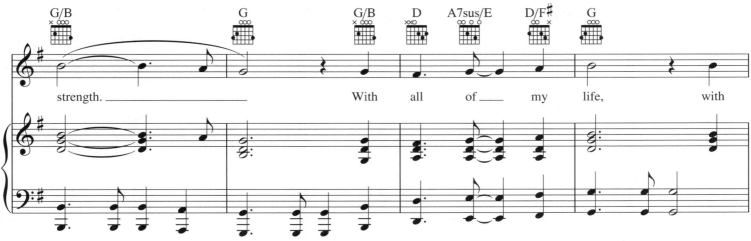

strength. _____ With all of ___ my life, with

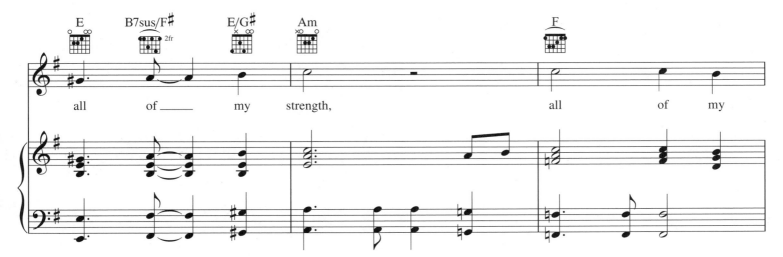

all of ___ my strength, all of my

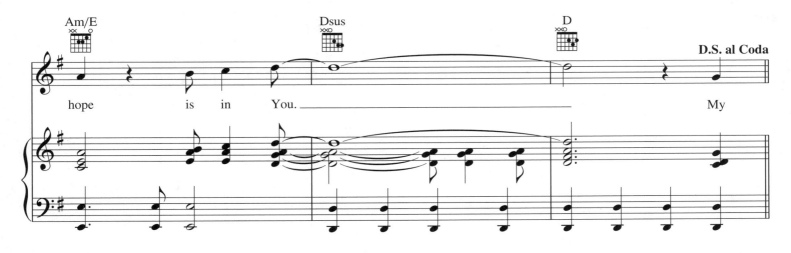

hope is in You. _____ My

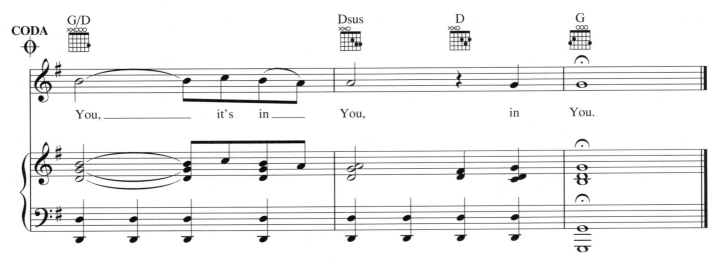

You, _____ it's in ___ You, in You.

MORE LOVE TO THEE

Words by ELIZABETH PAYSON PRENTISS
Music by WILLIAM H. DOANE

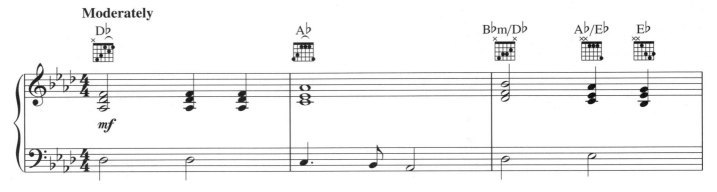

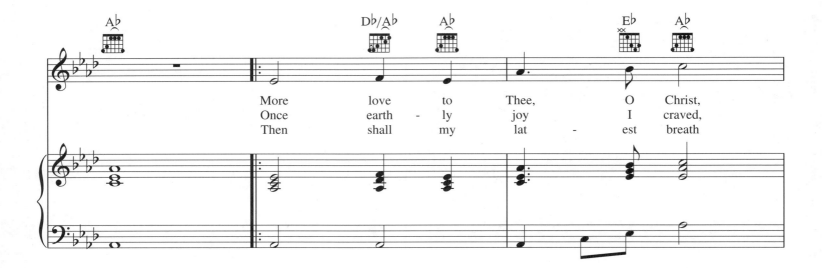

More love to Thee, O Christ,
Once earth - ly joy I craved,
Then shall my lat - est breath

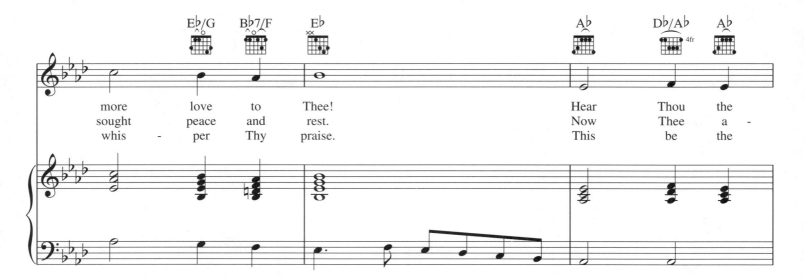

more love to Thee! Hear Thou the
sought peace and rest. Now Thee a -
whis - per and Thy praise. This be the

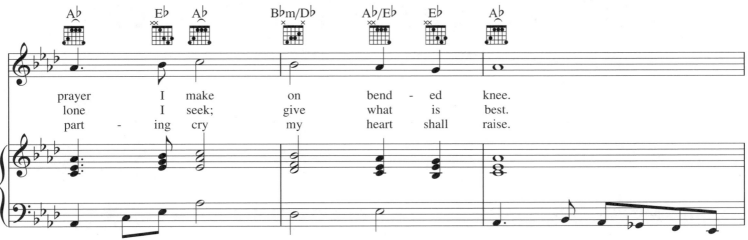

prayer   I make   on   bend - ed   knee.
lone   I seek;   give   what   is   best.
part - ing cry   my   heart shall raise.

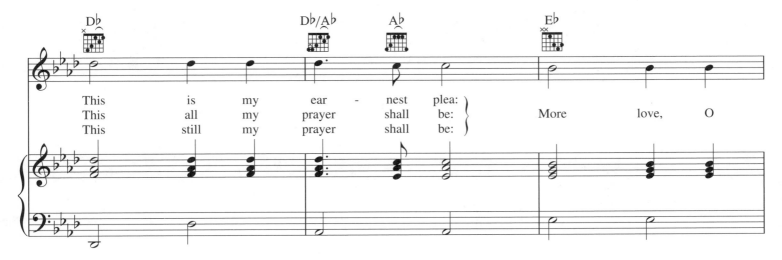

This   is   my   ear - nest plea:
This   all   my prayer shall be: } More   love,   O
This   still my prayer shall be:

Christ,   to Thee,   more   love   to   Thee,

more   love   to   Thee!   Thee!

MORE PRECIOUS THAN SILVER

Words and Music by
LYNN DeSHAZO

Warmly

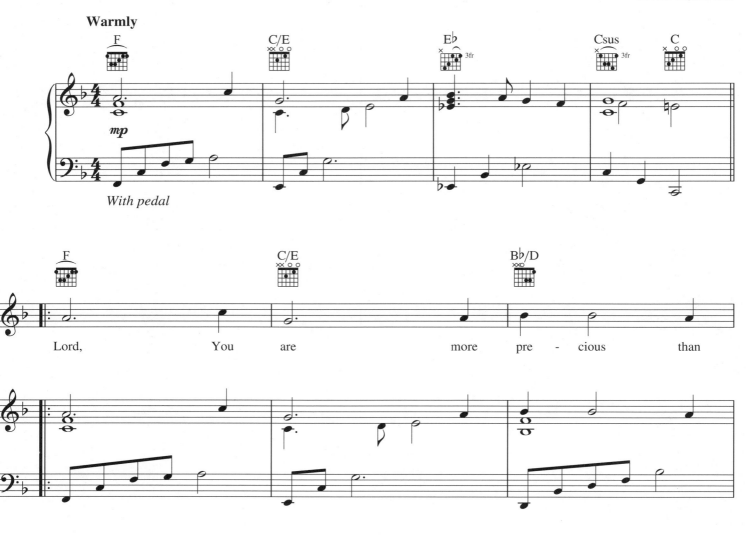

Lord, You are more pre - cious than sil - ver. Lord, You are more

cost - ly than gold. Lord, You

are more beau - ti - ful ___ than dia - monds, and

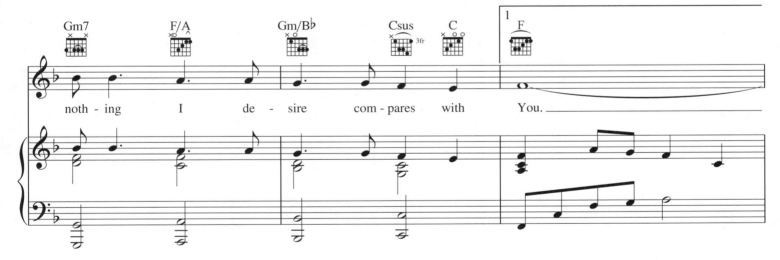

noth - ing I de - sire com - pares with You. ___

You. ___

MY JESUS, I LOVE THEE

Words by WILLIAM R. FEATHERSTON
Music by ADONIRAM J. GORDON

My Je- sus, I love Thee, I
love Thee be- cause Thou hast
love Thee in life, I will
man- sions of glo- ry and

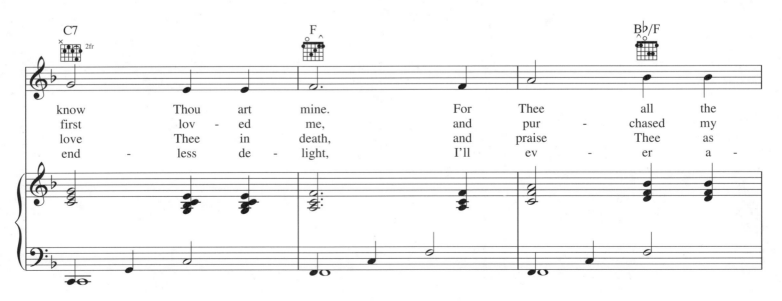

know Thou art mine. For Thee all the
first lov- ed me, and Thee pur- chased my
love Thee in death, and praise Thee as
end- less de- light, I'll ev- er a-

NO OTHER NAME

Words and Music by
ROBERT GAY

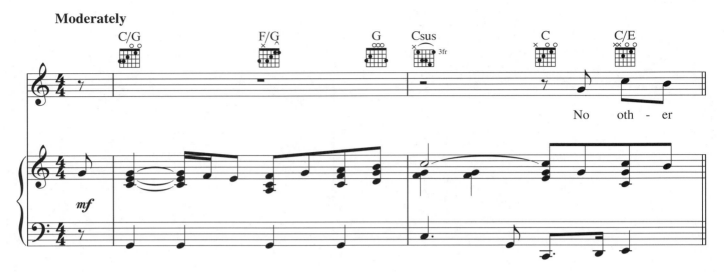

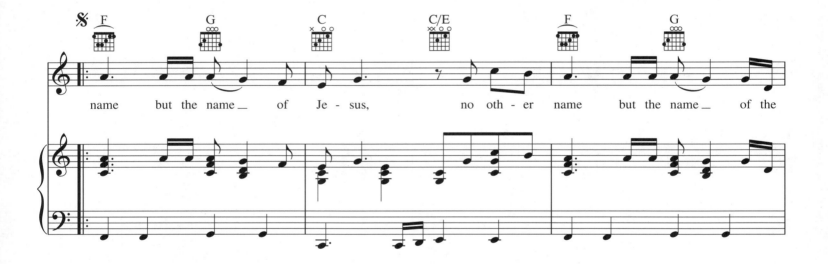

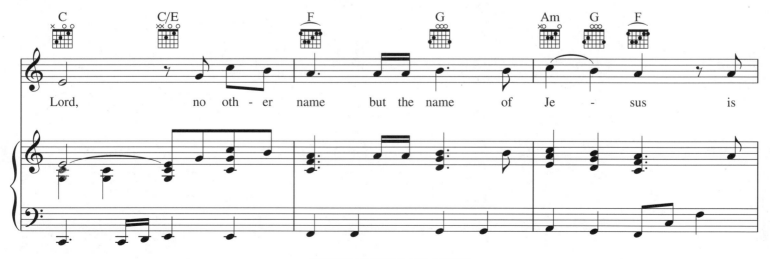

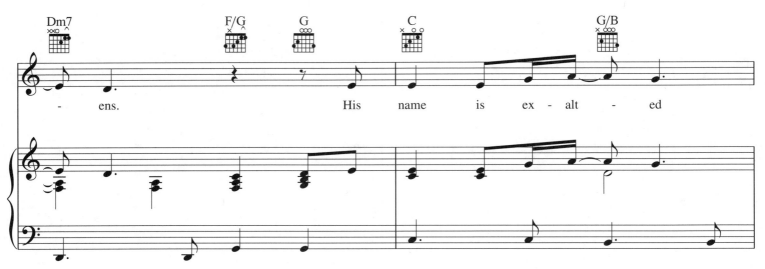

-ens. His name is ex - alt - ed

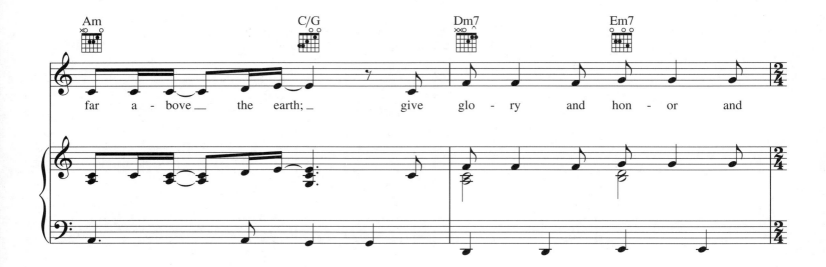

far a - bove __ the earth; __ give glo - ry and hon - or and

D.S. al Coda
(with repeat)

prais - es to His name. No oth - er

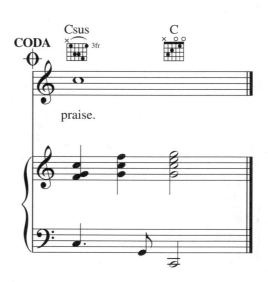

praise.

PRAISE HIM! PRAISE HIM!

Words by FANNY J. CROSBY
Music by CHESTER G. ALLEN

Hail Him, Hail Him, high - est arch - an - gels in
He, our Rock, our hope of e - ter - nal sal -
Je - sus, Sav - ior, reign - eth for - ev - er and

glo - ry; Strength and hon - or
va - tion; Hail Him! Hail Him!
ev - er; Crown Him! Crown Him!

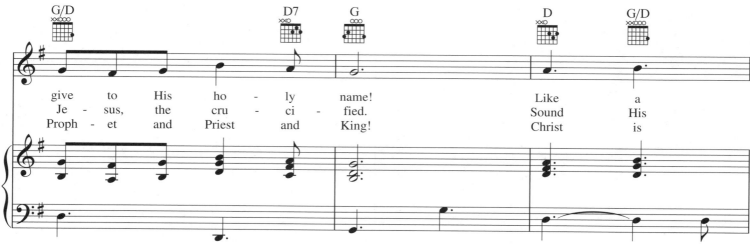

give to His ho - ly name! Like a
Je - sus, the cru - ci - fied. Sound His
Proph - et and Priest and King! Christ is

shep - herd, Je - sus will guard His chil - dren;
prais - es, Je - sus who bore our sor - rows;
com - ing, o - ver the world vic - to - rious;

O FOR A THOUSAND TONGUES TO SING

Words by CHARLES WESLEY
Music by CARL G. GLÄSER

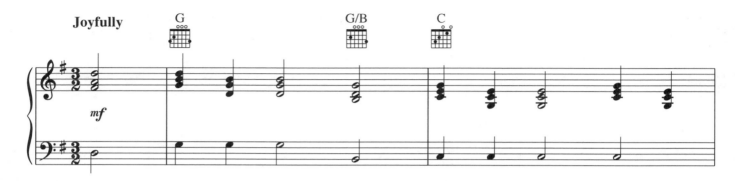

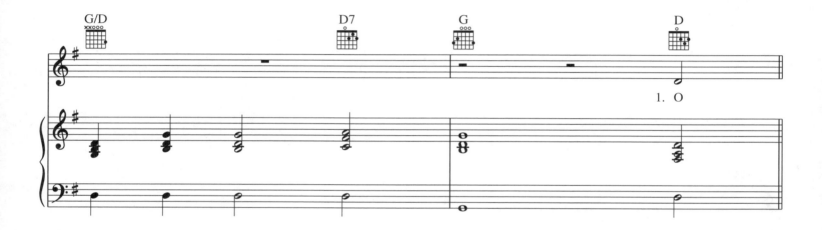

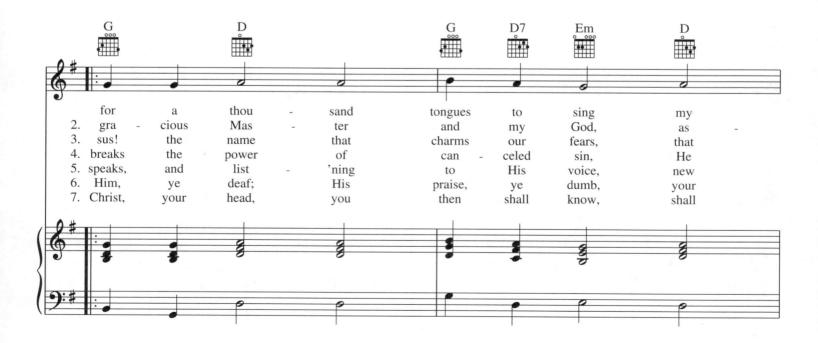

	for	a	thou - sand	tongues	to	sing	my
2.	gra -	cious	Mas -	ter	and	my	God,	as -
3.	sus!	the	name	that	charms	our	fears,	that
4.	breaks	the	power	of	can - celed	sin,	He
5.	speaks,	and	list -	'ning	to	His	voice,	new
6.	Him,	ye	deaf;	His	praise,	ye	dumb,	your
7.	Christ,	your	head,	you	then	shall	know,	shall

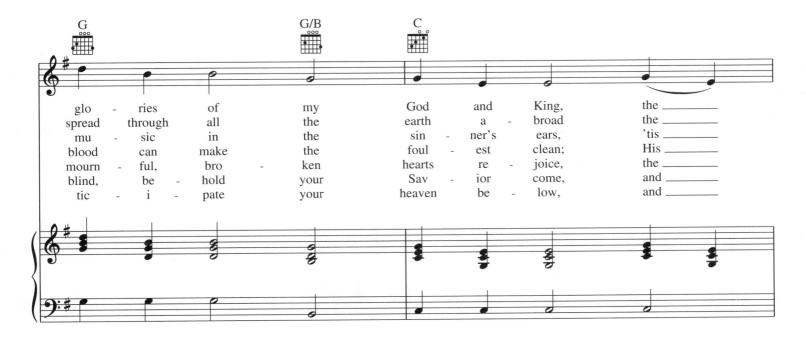

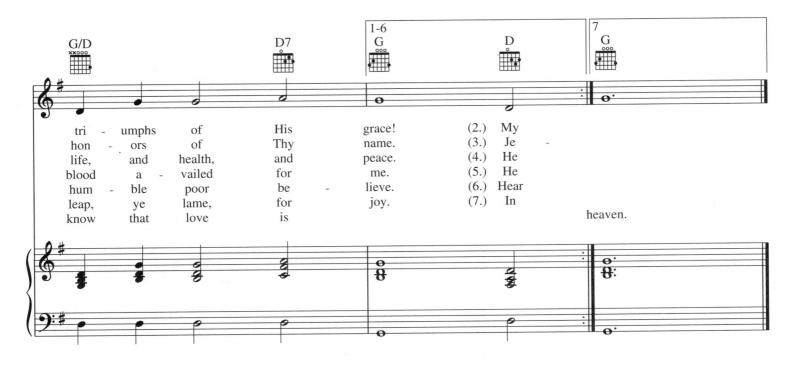

O WORSHIP THE KING

Words by ROBERT GRANT
Music attributed to JOHANN MICHAEL HAYDN
Arranged by WILLIAM GARDINER

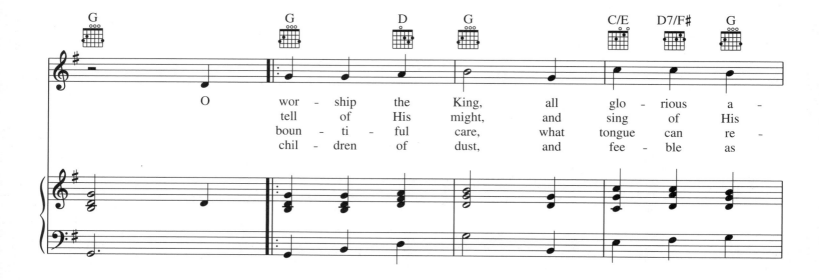

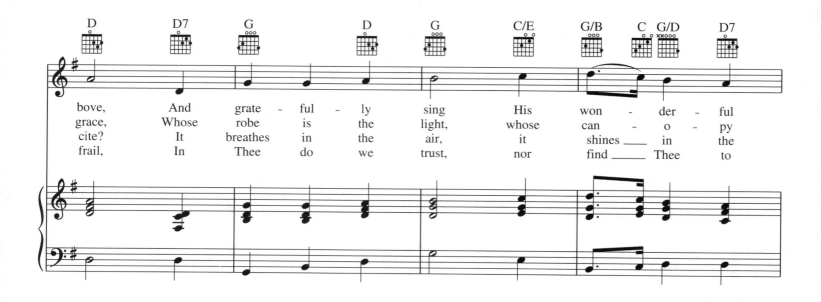

Lyrics:

O wor-ship the King, all glo-rious a-bove,
And grate-ful-ly sing His won-der-ful

tell of His might, and sing of His grace,
Whose robe is the light, whose can-o-py

boun-ti-ful care, what tongue can re-cite?
It breathes in the air, it shines in the

chil-dren of dust, and fee-ble as frail,
In Thee do we trust, nor find Thee to

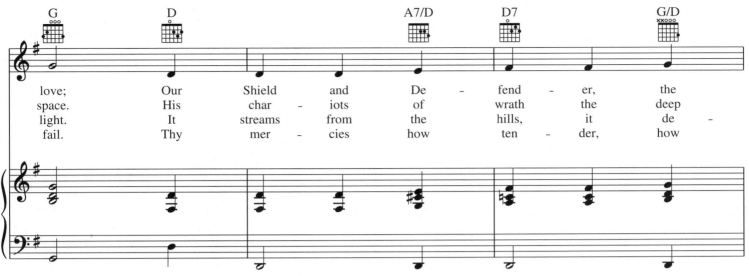

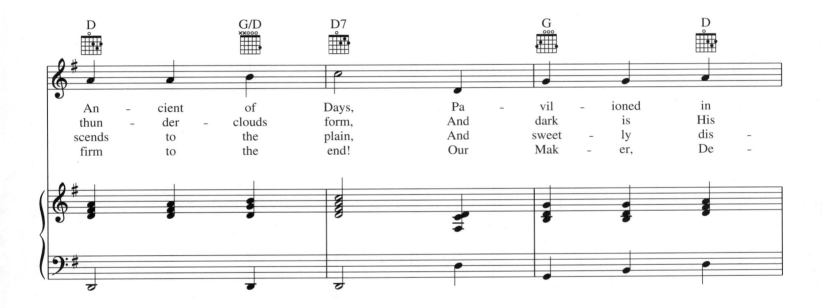

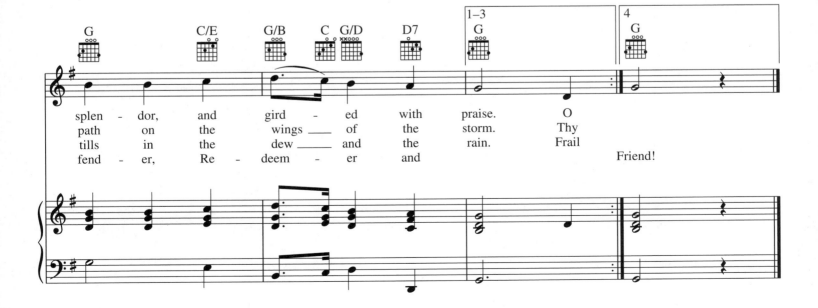

OPEN THE EYES OF MY HEART

Words and Music by
PAUL BALOCHE

Medium bright Pop

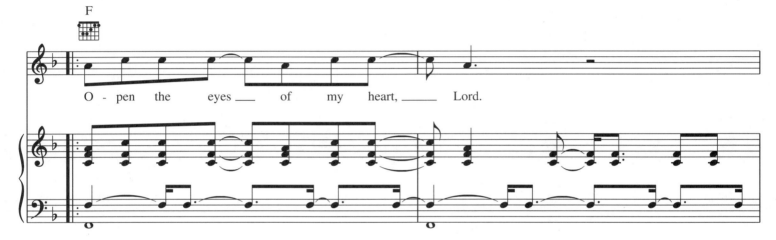

O- pen the eyes ___ of my heart, ___ Lord.

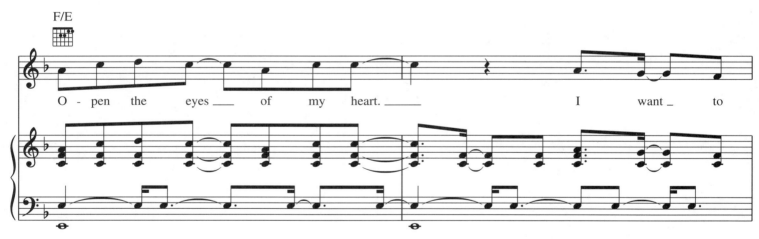

O- pen the eyes ___ of my heart. ___ I want _ to

see _____ You. _ I want _ to see ___ You. _

Fsus · F

O - pen the eyes ___ of my heart, ___

F/E

___ Lord.

O - pen the eyes ___ of my heart. ___

B♭sus2

I want ___ to see ___ You. ___

F

I want ___ to see ___ You, _

to see You _

high and lift - ed up, shin -

- ing in the light of Your glo - ry.

Pour out _ Your pow - er and love ___ as we sing ho - ly, ho - ly, ho -

- ly. _____

Pour out ___ Your pow - er and love ___ as we sing

ho - ly ho - ly, ho - ly. ___

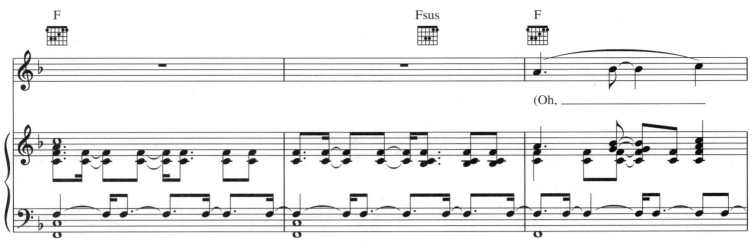

(Oh, _____

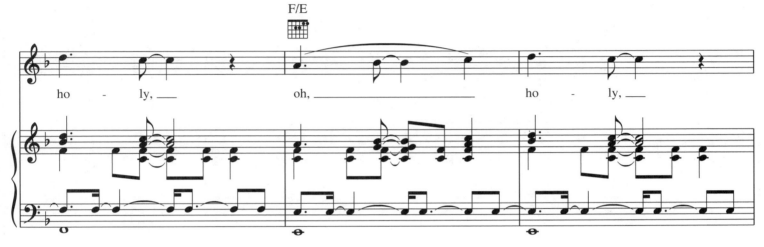

ho - ly, ___ oh, _____ ho - ly, ___

oh, _____ ho - ly, I want _ to see You.) _

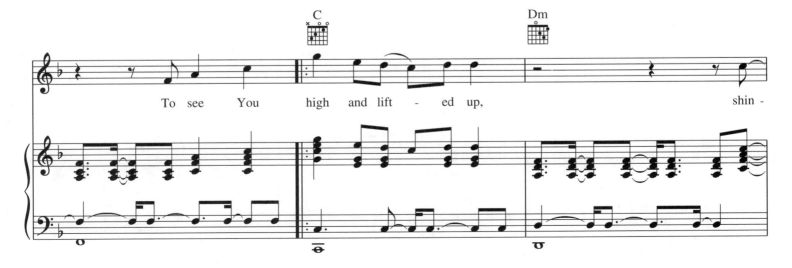

To see You high and lift - ed up, shin -

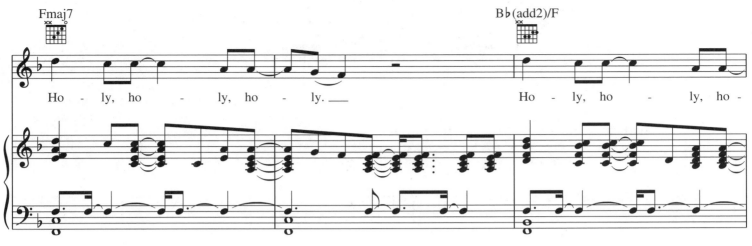

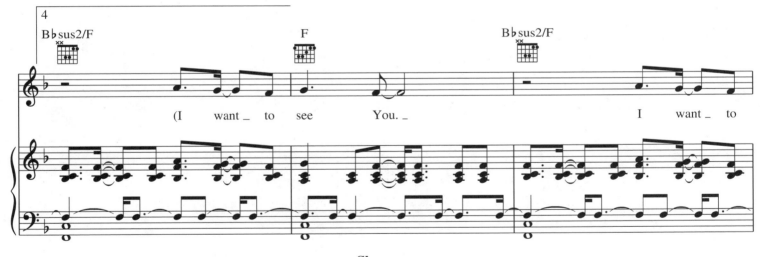

PRAISE TO THE LORD, THE ALMIGHTY

Words by JOACHIM NEANDER
Translated by CATHERINE WINKWORTH
Music from *Erneuerten Gesangbuch*

With strength

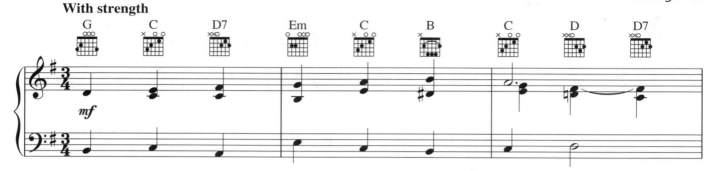

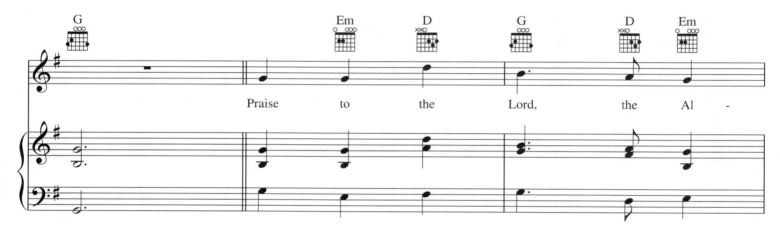

Praise to the Lord, the Al -

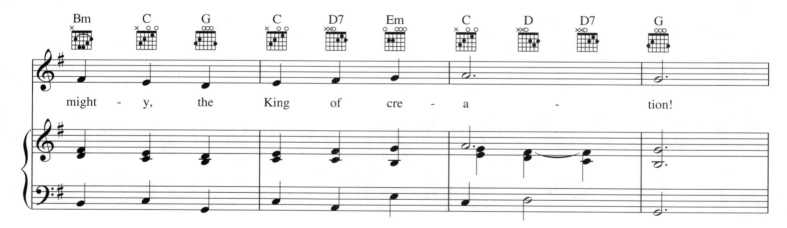

might - y, the King of cre - a - tion!

O my soul, praise Him, for He is thy health and sal -

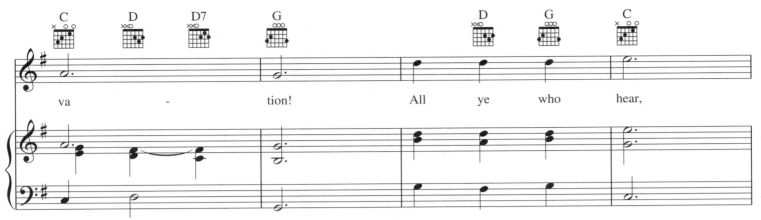

va - tion! All ye who hear,

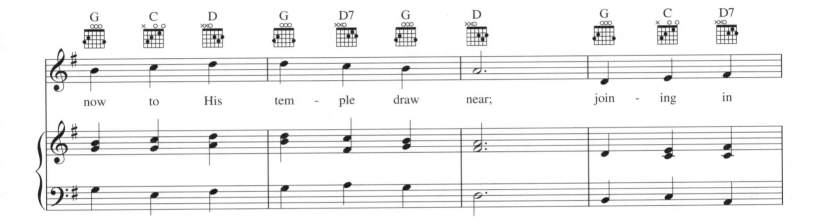

now to His tem - ple draw near; join - ing in

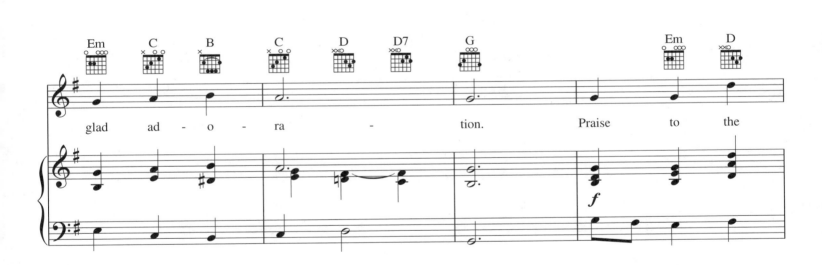

glad ad - o - ra - tion. Praise to the

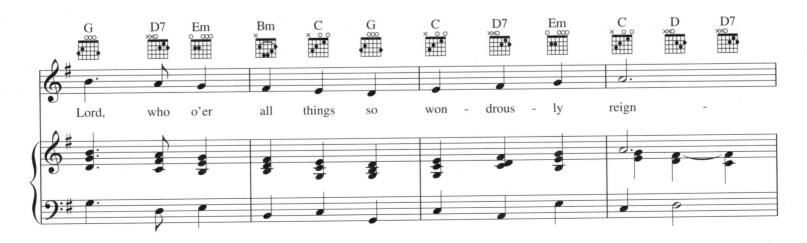

Lord, who o'er all things so won - drous - ly reign -

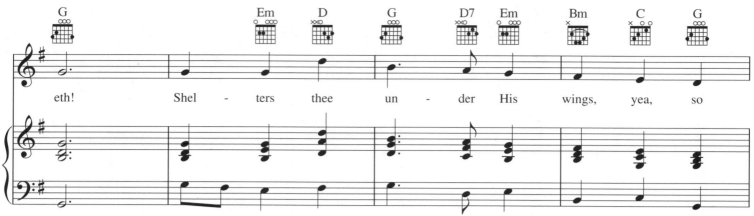

eth! Shel - ters thee un - der His wings, yea, so

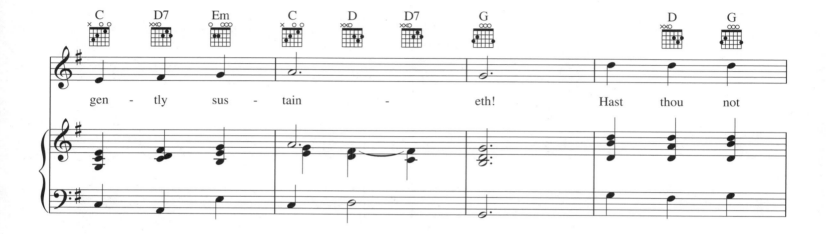

gen - tly sus - tain - eth! Hast thou not

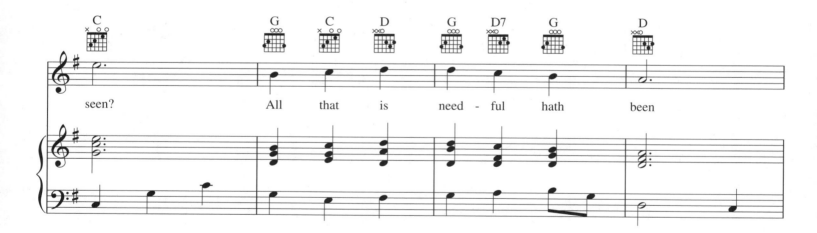

seen? All that is need - ful hath been

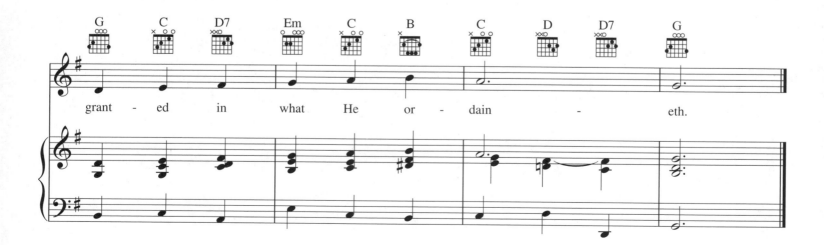

grant - ed in what He or - dain - eth.

SHINE, JESUS, SHINE

Words and Music by
GRAHAM KENDRICK

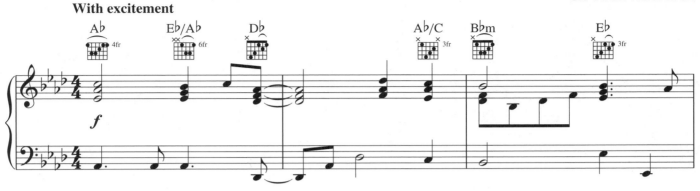

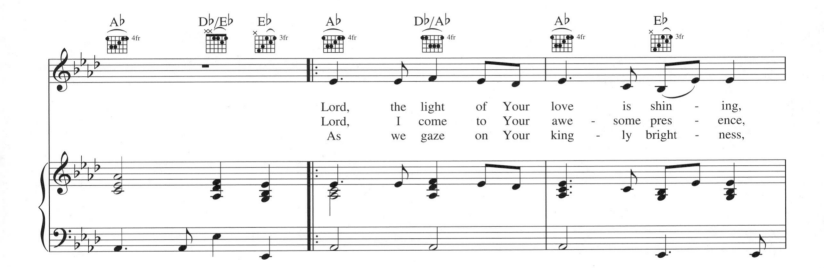

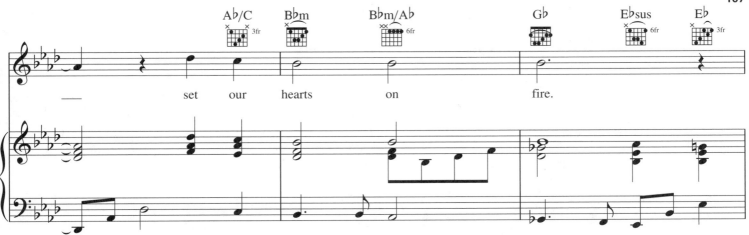

set our hearts on fire.

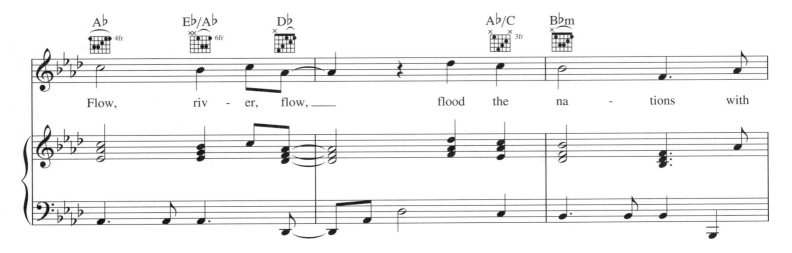

Flow, riv - er, flow, ___ flood the na - tions with

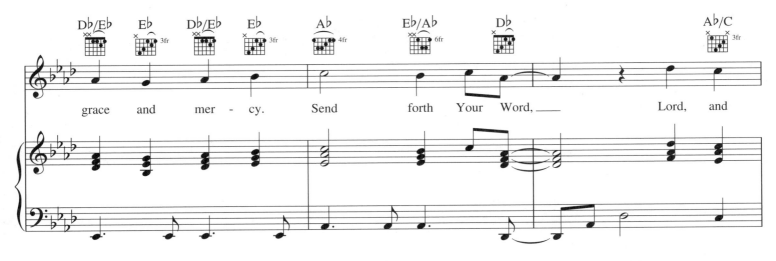

grace and mer - cy. Send forth Your Word, ___ Lord, and

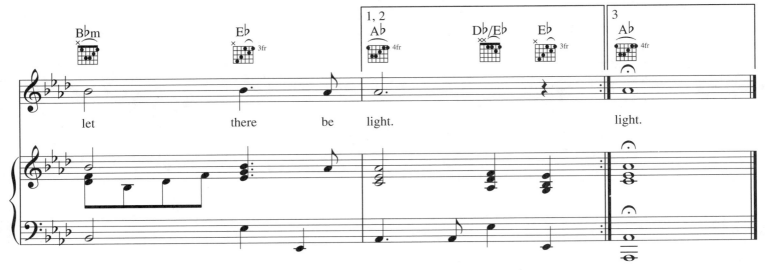

let there be light.

1, 2

light.

3

SANCTUARY

Words and Music by JOHN THOMPSON
and RANDY SCRUGGS

Moderately slow

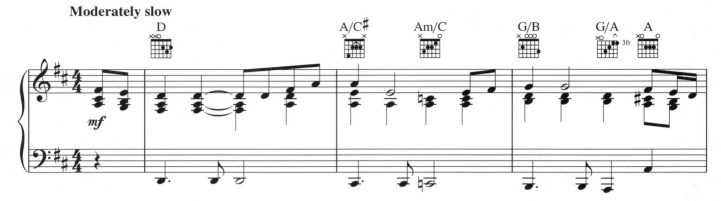

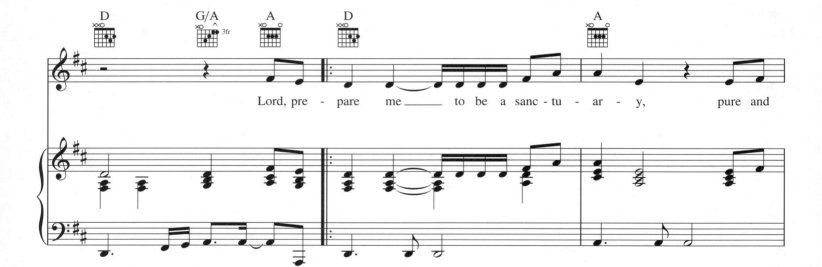

Lord, pre - pare me _____ to be a sanc - tu - ar - y, pure and

ho - ly, tried and true. _____ With thanks - giv - ing, I'll be a

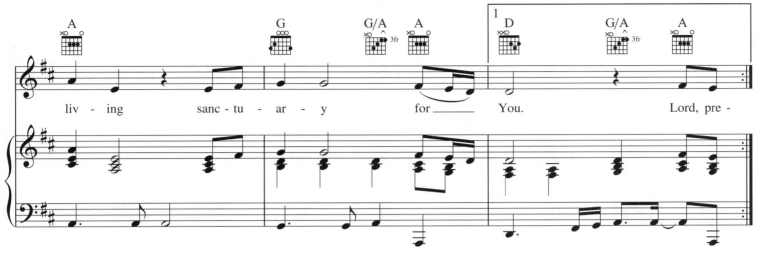

liv - ing sanc-tu - ar - y for ___ You. Lord, pre -

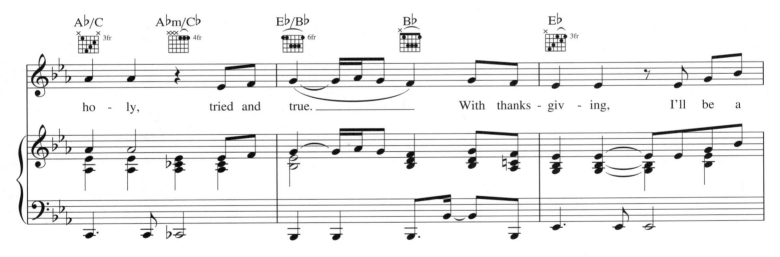

You. Lord, pre - pare me ___ to be a sanc-tu - ar - y, pure and

ho - ly, tried and true. ___ With thanks-giv - ing, I'll be a

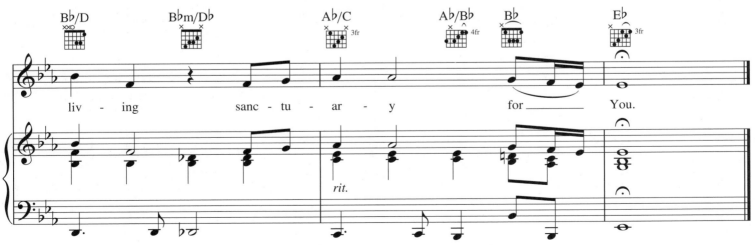

liv - ing sanc-tu - ar - y for ___ You.

rit.

SHINE ON US

Words and Music by MICHAEL W. SMITH
and DEBBIE SMITH

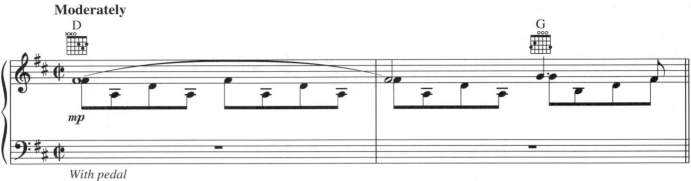

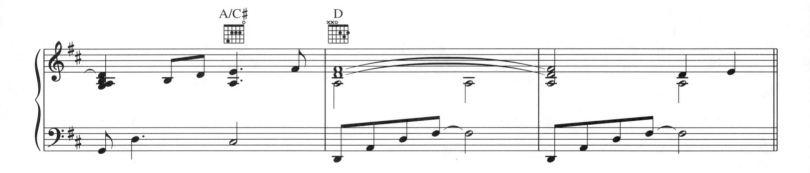

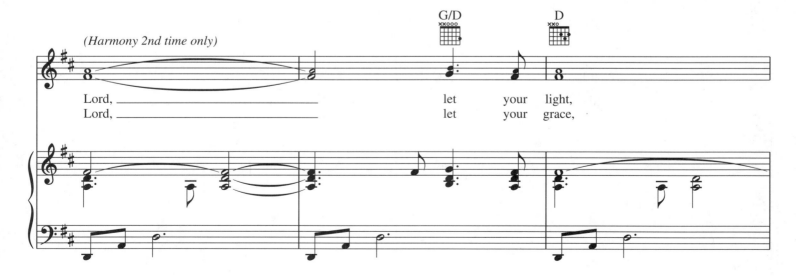

Lord, _____ let your light,

Lord, _____ let your grace,

SPIRIT OF THE LIVING GOD

Words and Music by DANIEL IVERSON
and LOWELL ALEXANDER

SHOUT TO THE LORD

Words and Music by
DARLENE ZSCHECH

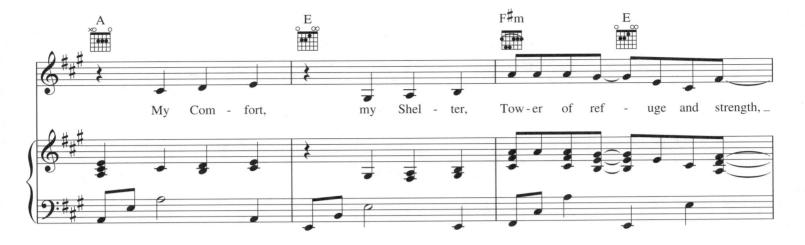

My Com - fort, my Shel - ter, Tow - er of ref - uge and strength, ___

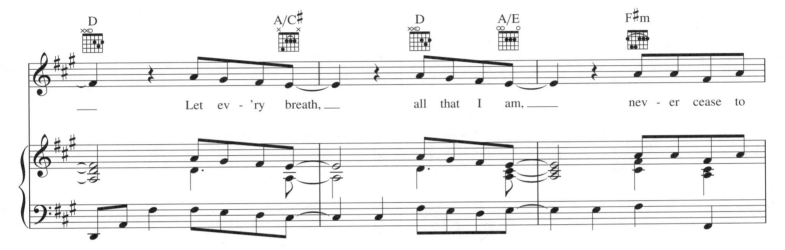

___ Let ev - 'ry breath, ___ all that I am, ___ nev - er cease to

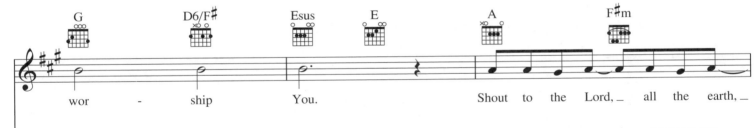

wor - ship You. Shout to the Lord, ___ all the earth, ___

___ let us sing; ___ pow - er and maj - es - ty, praise ___ to the King! ___

To Coda

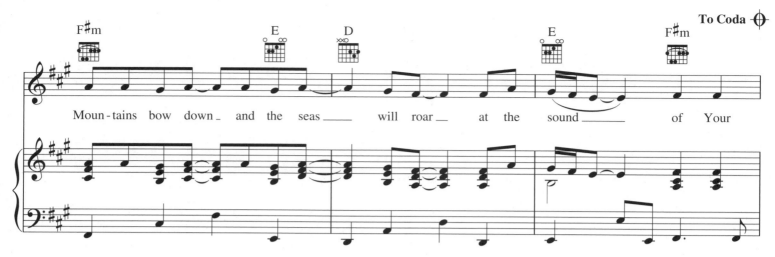

Moun-tains bow down _ and the seas ___ will roar _ at the sound ___ of Your

name. ___ I sing for joy _ at the work _ of Your hands, _ for-

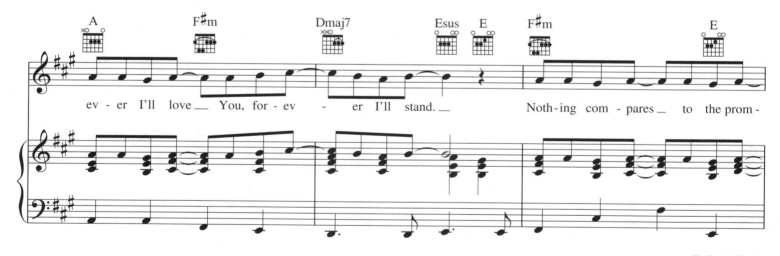

ev - er I'll love _ You, for-ev - er I'll stand. _ Noth-ing com-pares _ to the prom-

D.S. al Coda

- ise I have _ in You.

name._____ I sing for joy __ at the work ___ of Your hands, __ for-

ev - er I'll love __ You, for - ev - er I'll stand. __ Noth-ing com - pares __ to the prom-

- ise I have __ in, noth - ing com - pares __ to the prom - ise I have __ in,

noth - ing com - pares __ to the prom - ise I have __ in You._____

SPIRIT OF GOD, DESCEND UPON MY HEART

Words by GEORGE CROLY
Music by FREDERICK COOK ATKINSON

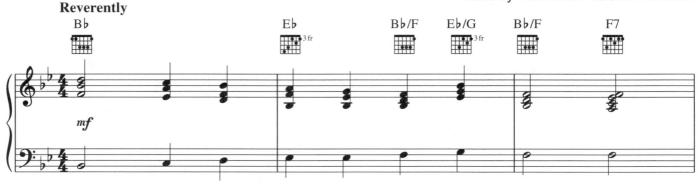

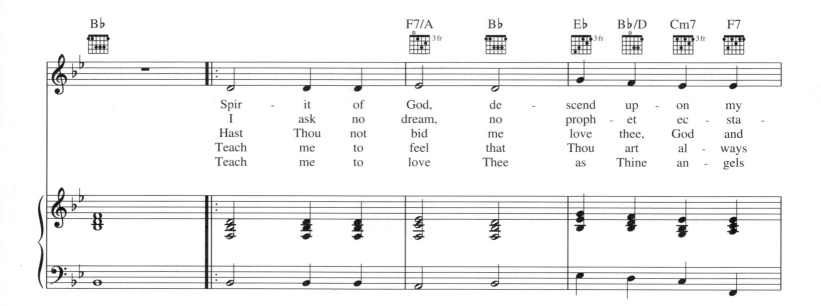

Spir - it of God, de - scend up - on my
I ask no dream, no proph - et ec - sta -
Hast Thou not bid me love thee, God and
Teach me to feel that Thou art al - ways
Teach me to love Thee as Thine an - gels

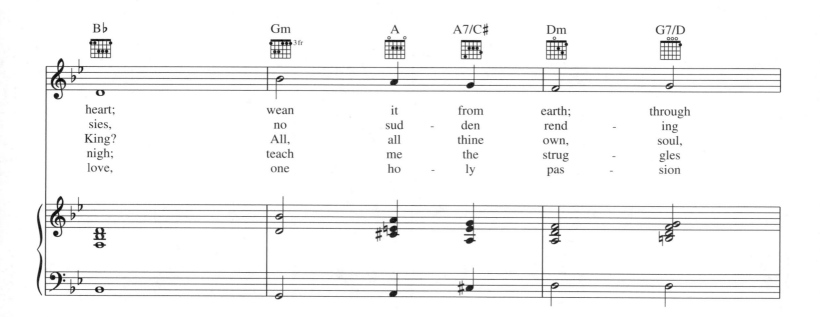

heart; wean it from earth; through
sies, no sud - den rend - ing
King? All, all thine own, soul,
nigh; teach me the strug - gles
love, one ho - ly pas - sion

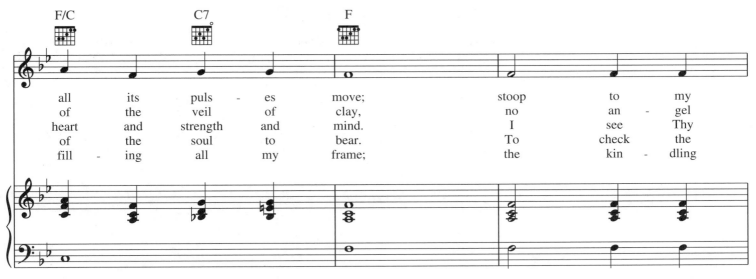

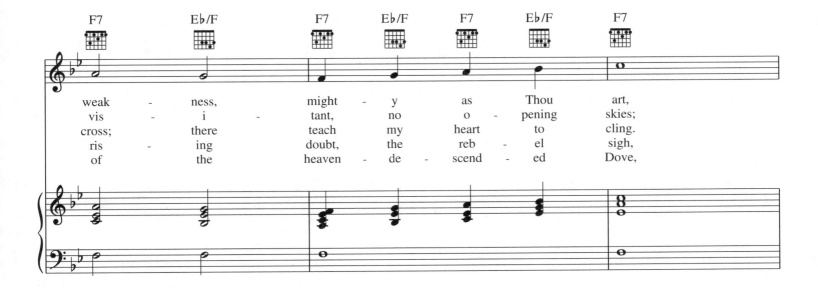

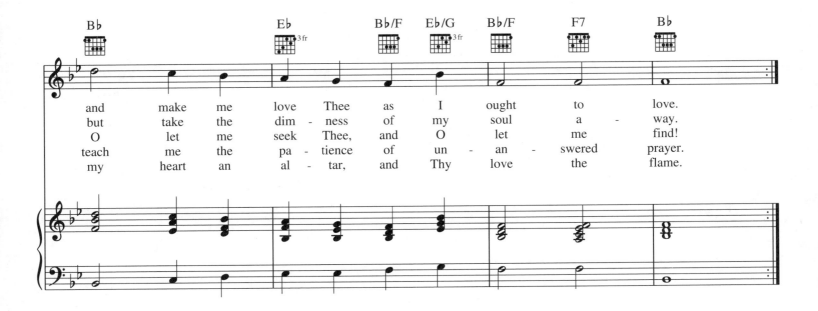

STEP BY STEP

Words and Music by
DAVID STRASSER "BEAKER"

Moderately fast

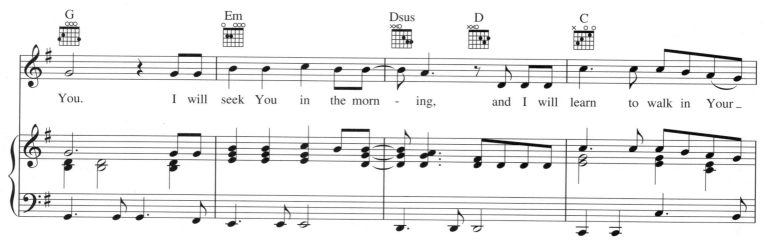

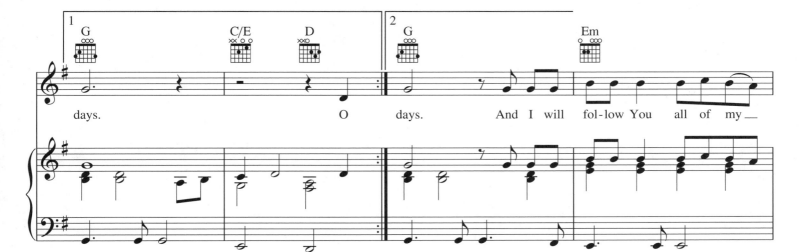

SWEET, SWEET SPIRIT

By DORIS AKERS

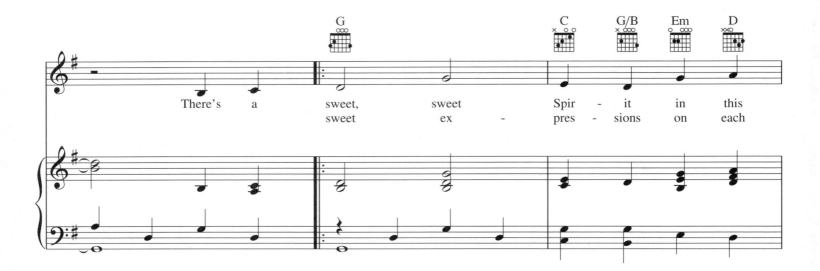

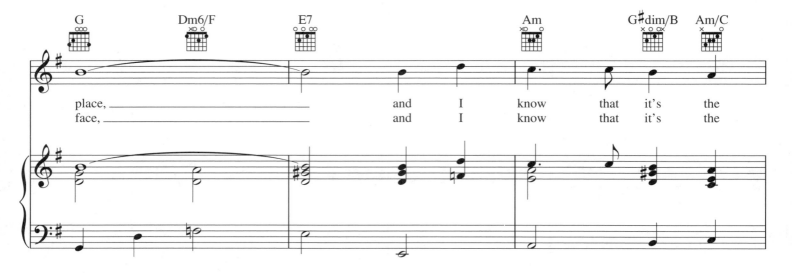

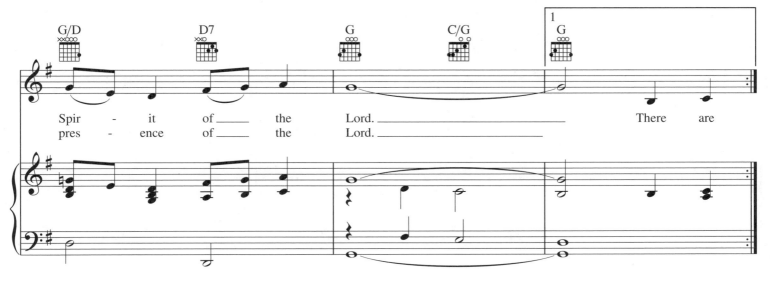

Spir - it of _____ the Lord. _____ There are
pres - ence of _____ the Lord. _____

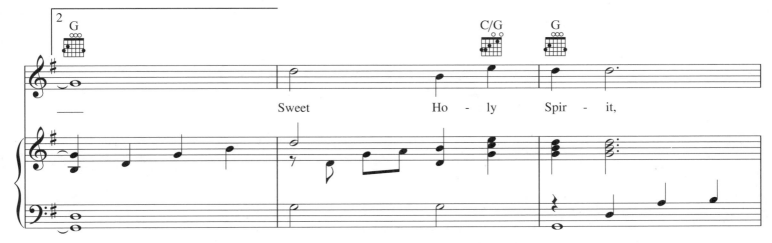

_____ Sweet Ho - ly Spir - it,

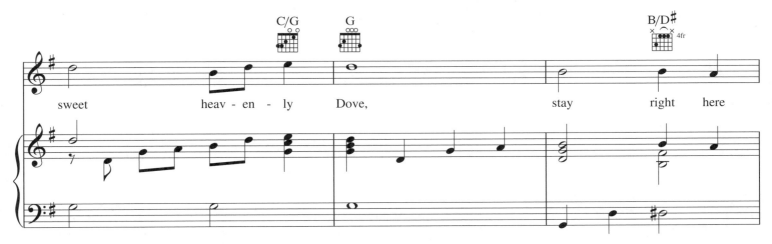

sweet heav - en - ly Dove, stay right here

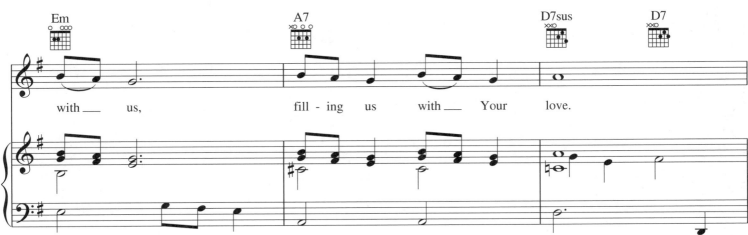

with _____ us, fill - ing us with _____ Your love.

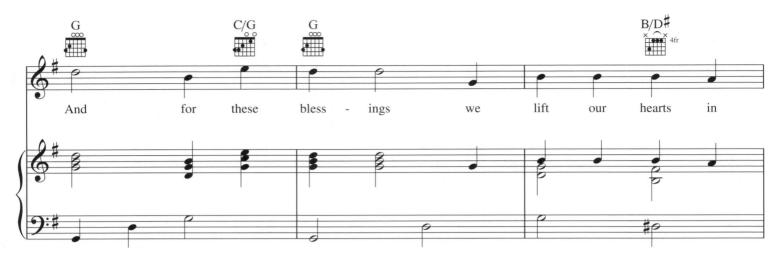

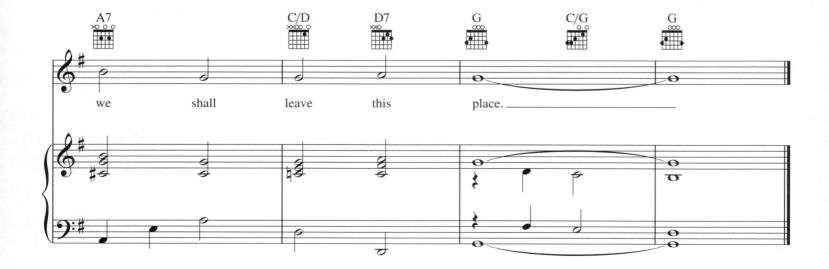

TAKE MY LIFE AND LET IT BE

Words by FRANCES R. HAVERGAL
Music by HENRY A. César MALAN

THERE IS A REDEEMER

Words and Music by
MELODY GREEN

Moderately

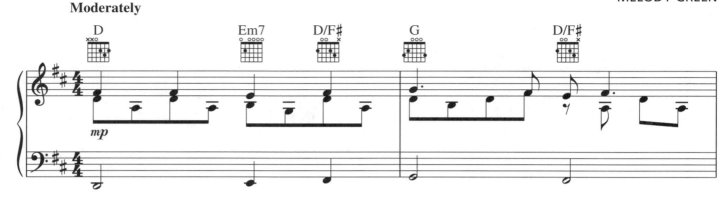

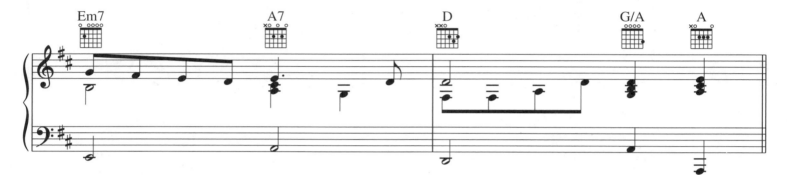

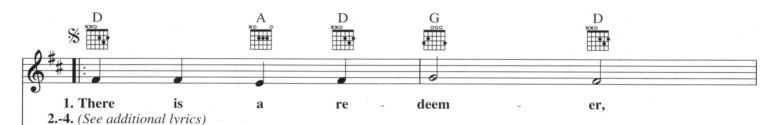

1. There is a re-deem - er,
2.-4. *(See additional lyrics)*

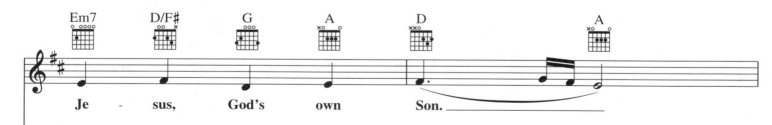

Je - sus, God's own Son. _____

Additional Lyrics

2. Jesus, my redeemer,
   Name above all names.
   Precious Lamb of God, Messiah,
   Oh, for sinners slain. *(To Chorus)*

3. When I stand in glory,
   I will see His face,
   And there I'll serve my King forever
   In that holy place. *(To Chorus)*

4. There is a redeemer,
   Jesus, God's own Son.
   Precious Lamb of God, Messiah,
   Holy One. *(To Chorus)*

TURN YOUR EYES UPON JESUS

Words and Music by
HELEN H. LEMMEL

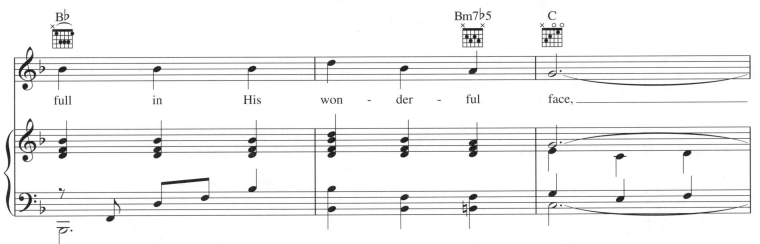

full in His won - der - ful face, _____

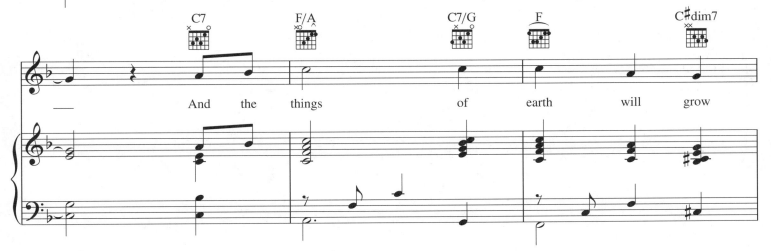

And the things of earth will grow

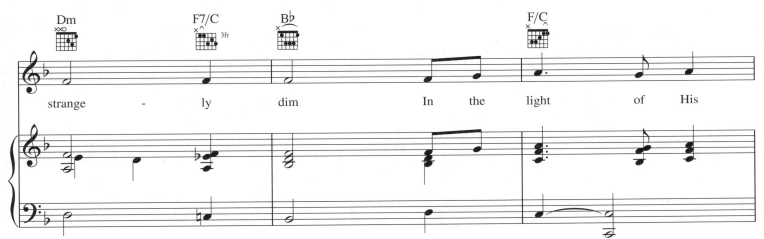

strange - ly dim In the light of His

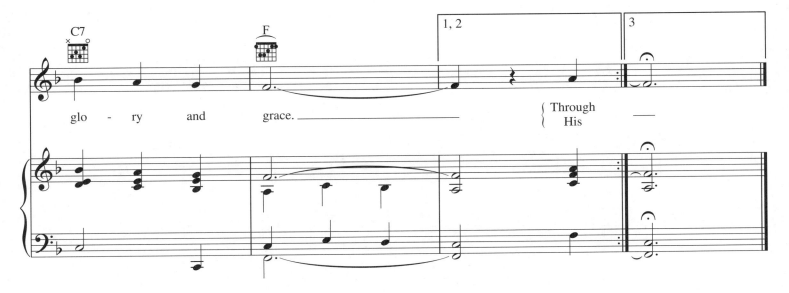

glo - ry and grace. _____

1, 2

3

{ Through
His

THIS IS THE DAY

By LES GARRETT

Joyfully

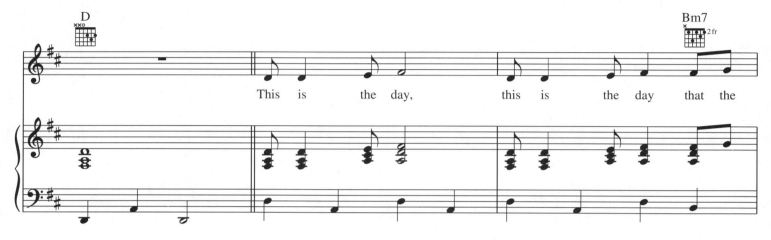

This is the day, this is the day that the

Lord has made, that the Lord has made.

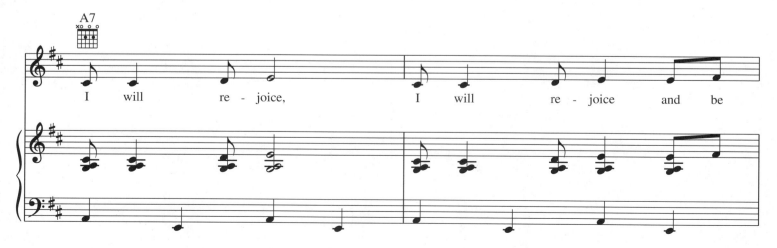

I will re-joice, I will re-joice and be

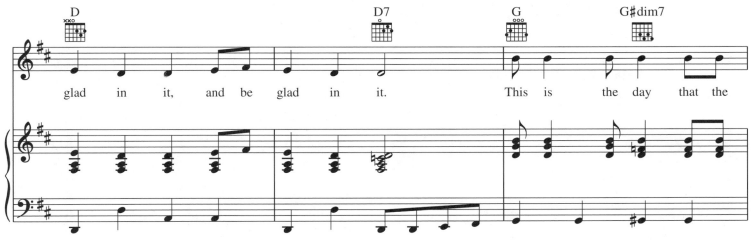

glad in it, and be glad in it. This is the day that the

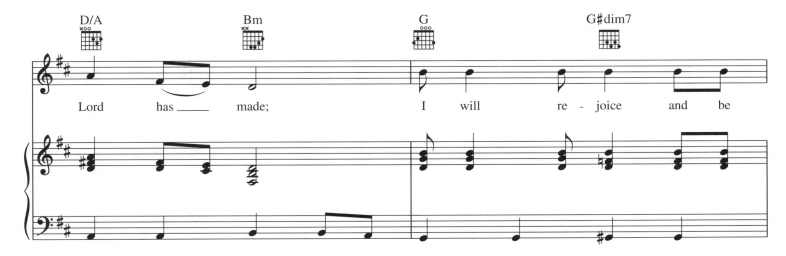

Lord has _____ made; I will re - joice and be

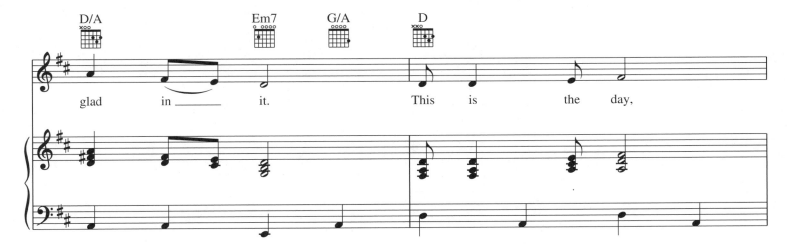

glad in _____ it. This is the day,

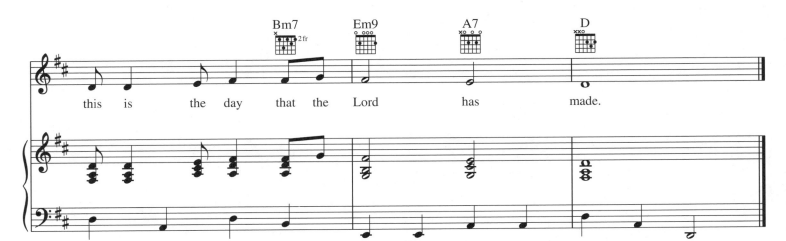

this is the day that the Lord has made.

TO GOD BE THE GLORY

Words by FANNY J. CROSBY
Music by WILLIAM H. DOANE

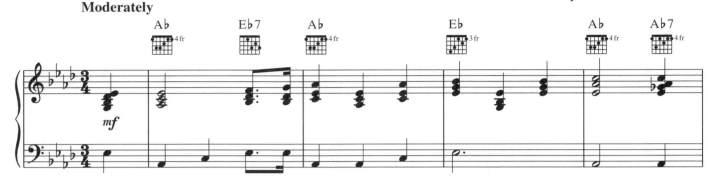

To God be the
per - fect re -
things He hath

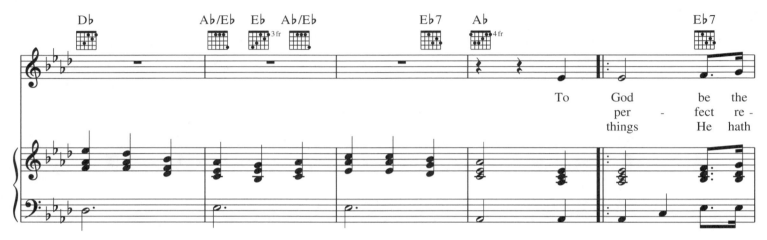

glo - ry, great things He hath done! so loved He the world that He gave us His
demp - tion, the pur - chase of blood, to ev - 'ry be - liev - er the prom - ise of
taught us, great things He hath done, and great our re - joic - ing through Je - sus the

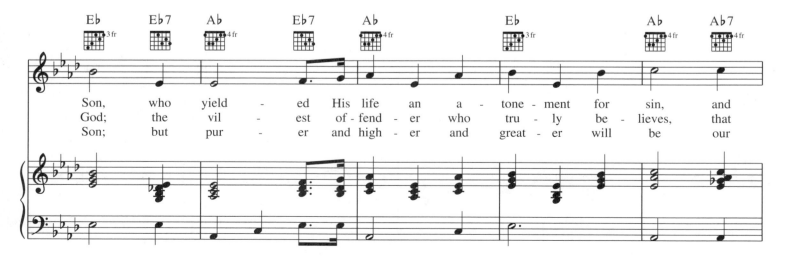

Son, who yield - ed His life an a - tone - ment for sin, and
God; the vil - est of - fend - er who tru - ly be - lieves, and that
Son; but pur - er and high - er and great - er will be our

WORTHY, YOU ARE WORTHY

Words and Music by
DON MOEN

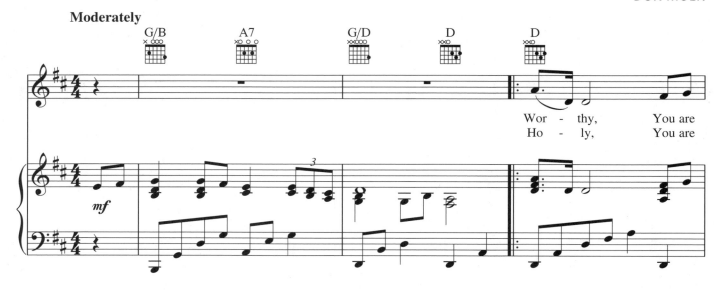

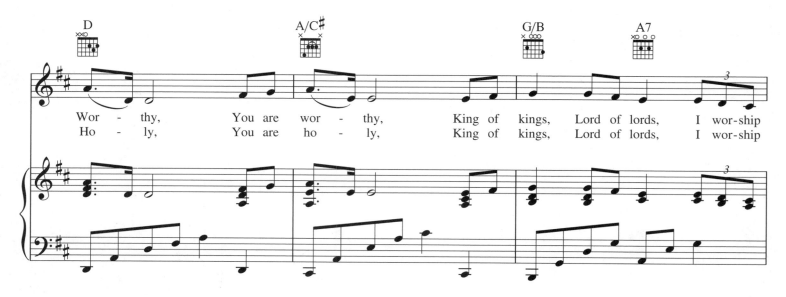

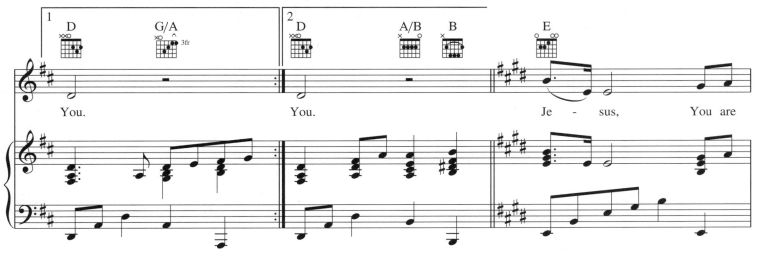

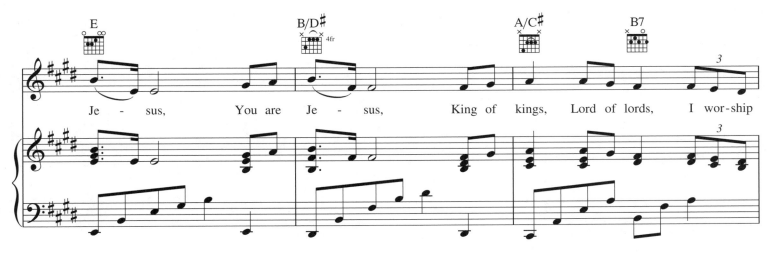

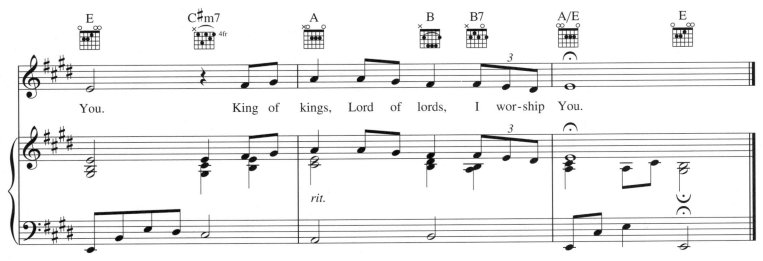

THE WONDERFUL CROSS

Words and Music by JESSE REEVES,
CHRIS TOMLIN and J.D. WALT

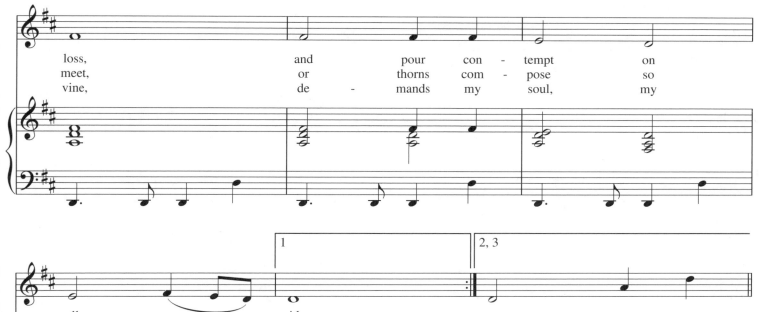

loss,
meet,
vine,

and
or
de -

pour
thorns
mands

con -
com -
my

tempt
pose
soul,

on
so
my

1

all
rich
life,

my
a
my

pride.

2, 3

crown?
all.

O

the

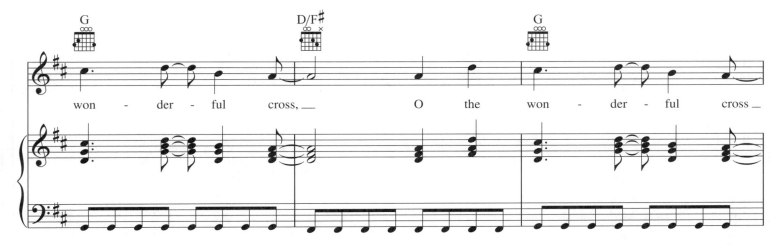

| G | D/F# | G |

won - der - ful cross, ___ O the won - der - ful cross ___

| D/F# | G | D/F# |

___ bids ___ me come ___ and die ___ and find ___ that ___ I ___ may tru -

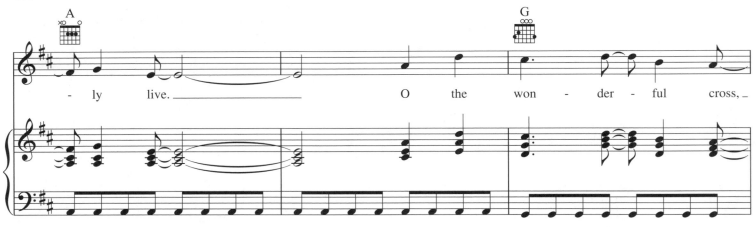

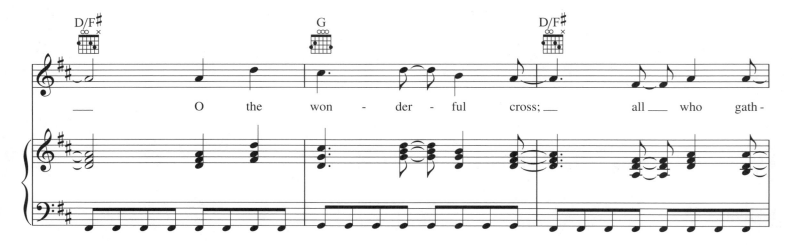

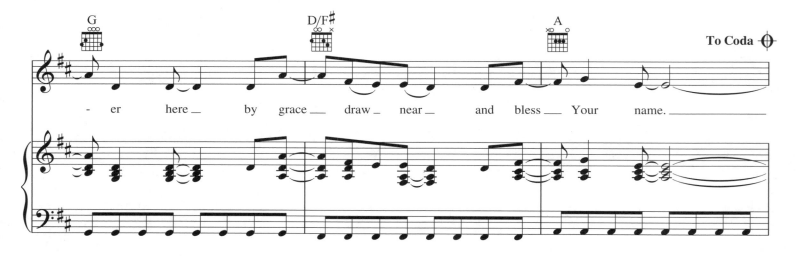

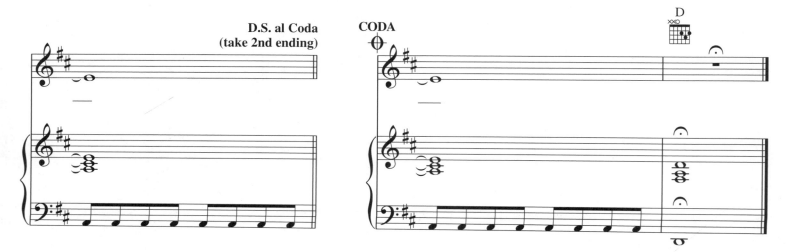